ONE WORLD
IN THE MAKING

ONE WORLD
IN THE MAKING

By

Ralph Barton Perry

PROFESSOR OF PHILOSOPHY,
HARVARD UNIVERSITY

NEW YORK
CURRENT BOOKS, INC.
A. A. WYN, Publisher
1945

Core
EI

First Edition

THIS BOOK IS DEDICATED TO THE MEMORY OF

WENDELL WILLKIE

the First Private Citizen of that ONE WORLD Which Having Discovered for Himself He Disclosed to His Fellow-Americans

CONTENTS

Contents

Contents

PREFACE

THIS book is the outgrowth of a series of public lectures delivered before the Lowell Institute in Boston in March 1945. To the officers of the Lowell Institute I hereby tender my grateful acknowledgment. As I review the several chapters of the book I am appalled at their seeming pretentiousness. They traverse almost all the fields of human learning, each of which has its vast literature, and its corps of experts. These experts have a decent respect for one another's territories. Only a philosopher would rush into them all—where experts fear to tread—only a philosopher and the general public. That I hope will be a bond between the author and his readers. I, too, on most of the questions here considered, belong to the general public, and speak as one member of the general public to another.

For this, as for most of my books, I am largely indebted to two remarkable institutions—the university and the secretary—which resemble one another in a generosity which asks no credit. The university is Harvard, and the secretary is Mrs. Catherine F. Malone. Neither can be repaid. My gratitude to them is not repayment, but an acknowledgment of its impossibility.

Ralph Barton Perry

Cambridge, Massachusetts
June 1, 1945

CHAPTER ONE

What It Takes to Make a World

IN HIS famous book entitled *One World,* that great world citizen Wendell Willkie gave expression at one and the same time to several ideas. He conceived the world as one because he had gone around it in forty-nine days, and had seen great stretches of its surface as a terrestrial landscape. At the same time his trip confirmed the belief, which he already held, that the recurrence of war could be prevented only if all the nations of the earth united to prevent it. Peace, he believed, must be global if it is to be durable. And at the same time he insisted that political arrangements would not suffice, even if supported by overwhelming force. There must also be economic solidarity, and economic progress embracing the so-called backward peoples of the earth. He might have added, and no doubt would have agreed, that there must be some degree of global solidarity in every field of human interest and endeavor—not political and economic merely, but moral, legal, cultural, educational, and religious.

It will appear that there are two fundamentally different meanings of "one world." There is that oneness of the world which has already come to pass—a oneness of contact and interdependence brought about mainly by scientific and technological changes; and there is that oneness of the world which has yet to be achieved by organization and institutions. The first unity sets the stage for the second in making it both necessary and possible. That these two unities are not the same is proved by the present war, which is an effect of the first unity in the absence of the second. Contact and interdependence create a problem which if not solved results in destruction; but which if solved will result in constructive good surpassing any which mankind has yet achieved.

The present chapter is devoted to that unity of contact and interdependence which is already a fact. "One World" does not mean universe, in the sense of that totality of being which philosophy and religion from their earliest beginnings have served to emphasize. The reference is to that particular part of the universe which is inhabited by man during his mortal existence. "World" means "earth," or "this world," where men spend their threescore years and ten. And it means *man's* world, the world of his conscious life, and not the antecedent physical or natural order. The earth has its own characteristic unity. It is a sphere, revolving on its own axis, and moving as a unit in its own lonely and repeated journeys about the sun. Its oceans, lakes, rivers, harbors, plains and valleys, winds and ocean currents, bind the parts of this surface together at the same time that its mountain ranges, deserts, distances, and variable climates render its different regions relatively inaccessible. Its crust has evolved through the astronomical and geological ages until it has become fit to sustain that elaborate and delicately balanced form of life represented by the human organism. The chemical composition of its soil, its solar light and heat, its mineral deposits, its molecular and atomic structures, its differences of altitude above sea level, provide latent energies and materials ready at hand for human use.

But this natural habitat, while it provides the indispensable physical conditions, is not what we mean when we speak of the growing unity of the world. We are thinking of a change that is measurable not in terms of astronomical or geological time, but in terms of the span of human history. We are thinking of the world which *man has made* and *is making* out of the opportunity which the more stable constitution of things has provided.

It is true that man has in some small degree remodeled the surface of the earth. He has dug ditches such as the Suez and Panama canals by which to create more direct passages from ocean to ocean; he has bored tunnels through mountain barriers, as in Switzerland; he has dredged harbors, and built dams by which to alter the courses of rivers. But these are trivial changes which would soon be effaced if man did not keep them in repair. On the whole, the surface of the earth constitutes a permanent environment to which man must adapt himself as best he can. The terrestrial unity which has developed progressively since the dawn of prehistory is the story of that adaptation, consisting of the furniture and the relationships which the human family has created. A cinematic foreshortening of this story, seen as a river against the unchanging configuration of its bed, reveals the continuous spreading and confluence of human life. From its first trickles and pools, whether from a single Garden of Eden or from separate evolutionary breeding grounds, the stream of human life is seen to flow into all parts of the earth's surface, like an inundation which overcomes barrier after barrier as its level rises.

To examine in sequence the various forces by which man has progressively occupied the surface of the earth, and come to be a single family living together under a common terrestrial roof, requires two broad correctives. In the first place, these forces, though they are distinguishable and must be divided for purposes of exposition, actually interact and work together in the course of history. No important step in the progression can be attributed to a single cause. In the second place, each of these forces has its divisive as well as its unifying effects, and when we speak of them as making for unity, we mean that this is their net effect. Each new achievement of unity has created new barriers and chasms; but in the long run and on the whole, the tunnels and the bridges have prevailed.

The first of the forces by which man has made his world one is *knowledge*. His earliest ideas sprang from his speculative and imaginative faculties, and assumed the form of myths, religious dogmas, or metaphysical systems. But these ideas were cosmic rather than terrestrial in their scope. Man *looked out from* earth rather than at it, and focused his attention on first causes and ultimate destiny rather than on the immediate scene of his mortal existence.

The story of man's growing knowledge of his earth turns, in the first place, on the gradual correction of appearances by scientific theory. The earth appears to be a flat, immovable disk, surrounded by water, which meets the dome of the sky at the horizon. Science now teaches that the earth is a sphere rotating on its axis, revolving about the sun, and moving with the solar system itself relatively to other celestial bodies. But while this state of affairs is many millions of years old as a matter of fact, it is barely thousands of years old as a matter of knowledge. In the European tradition the idea that the earth is a sphere dates from the sixth century B.C., and is still undergoing corrections. But the idea that the earth rotates on its axis and revolves about the sun did not win final acceptance among scientists until the sixteenth century A.D. It is, in short, less than five hundred years old.

If we turn from science to the perception of the layman, these ideas are still more recent. There is an immense difference between the theories of the scientist based upon experimentation, or mathematical calculation, and the look or feel of things to the average man. Long after science has recognized and transcended the relativities of appearance man himself continued to take them for absolutes. But when one observes ships hull down at sea, or sees the earth's shadow cast upon the moon, then one *experiences* the earth's curvature. If one circumnavigates the earth, one translates its spherical shape into practice. In proportion as this experience and practice are repeated and shared, and become more palpable, man can be said to *live* on a sphere.

In short, it is one thing that the earth should be spherical; another thing, separated by millions of years, that scientists should know it to be spherical, and that their students should then be able, when asked, to give the correct answer; and still another and extremely recent thing to perceive the earth's sphericity for oneself and execute it in action. And it is this last phase on which mankind is now entering, despite the fact that in the experience of most men of today the earth still seems incorrigibly flat.

It is to be noted that men have not yet reached this phase in respect to the motion of the earth. Despite the teachings of astronomy, the earth is still experienced as stationary. We still see the sun rising in the east, crossing the heavens, and setting in the west; and the whole panoply of heavenly bodies, including both planets and fixed stars, revolves about a fixed center where the human observer

stands. Not even the poet has yet enabled us to regard ourselves as passengers traveling through space at an appalling
speed in a direction compounded of diurnal rotation, annual revolution, and the journey of the solar system through
interstellar space at the rate of twelve miles a second.

In short, man is not yet completely domesticated in a
Copernican world. The great Alexandrian astronomers,
beginning with Hipparchus in the second century B.C. and
culminating with Ptolemy in the second century A.D., arranged the heavens and the earth in a pattern that endured
more than a thousand years. This Ptolemaic world coincided both with the order of appearance and with the
teaching of the Christian Scriptures. It was a cozy world
whose outer boundaries coincided with limits of human
vision, and in which the earth was the fixed and central
scene of the drama of human action and salvation, with
the heavens as a backdrop.

The new astronomy in which the earth became just another moving celestial body, one of insignificant size and
station, was profoundly shocking to every human habit
and prejudice. But as the dignity of the earth diminished,
its inhabitants became more, rather than less, aware of it.
The older astronomy made man cosmos-conscious rather
than earth-conscious. It directed his attention vertically toward heaven rather than horizontally toward his surrounding. As the heavens receded and merged with infinite and
unknown regions beyond, the earth began to fill their
place. Man's growing sense of cosmic homelessness heightened attachment to his terrestrial home. The earth became
his ship voyaging in vast, uncharted seas. He became increasingly conscious of his dependence on its support and
on its provisions, increasingly interested in its decks and

cabins and in the fellow passengers with whom he was thus cast adrift.

Man's growing acquaintance with the concrete details of the surface of the earth is called exploration. No doubt man has always been an explorer. Curiosity and greed have tempted him, danger, congestion, and want have driven him, to move across boundaries, to look beyond and peer behind. This has been perpetually true throughout history, and universally true of all human groups. As the Mediterranean peoples spread from their center, so did the inhabitants of the Americas, and of East Asia, and of the Pacific Islands, from theirs.

To trace discovery from the Mediterranean center is not, however, a mere parochialism. The Mediterranean peoples together with the Scandinavians and Germanic tribes to the north have been a peculiarly restless, mobile, enterprising, and intrusive lot. They have done the greater part of the interregional visiting. Greeks, Phoenicians, Romans, Arabs, and Norsemen in ancient and medieval times, followed later by Spaniards, Italians, Portuguese, Dutch, French, English, and Americans, possessed of every appropriate virtue and vice—courage, hardihood, cruelty, initiative, evangelism, invention, avarice, the spirit of rivalry, love of power, and love of the sea—have overrun the earth and suffered no alien place, however remote and inaccessible, to remain aloof. They have created itineraries, made contacts, drawn maps, and collected a vast and ever growing fund of information.

Great explorers and geographers, such as Eudoxus, Alexander and his generals, and Strabo, led the way in ancient times, and were followed in the Middle Ages by Eric the Red, Leif Ericson, Marco Polo, Ibn-Batuta, and the Crusaders. But beginning with the fifteenth century ex-

ploration was so accelerated, consolidated, and amply recorded as to mark an epoch. That unusual combination of
circumstances and release of human energies which we call
the Renaissance redirected human attention from the next
world to this, and sent man prying about with a new zest
and audacity. The pure spirit of exploration was epito-
mized by the Dutchman Van Linschoten, whose *Itinerario*,
published in 1595, contained the first European description of the Far East. "My heart is longing day and night,"
he said, "for voyages to far-away lands." * [1] This was the
age of Prince Henry the Navigator, Columbus, Magellan,
Amerigo Vespucci, Balboa, De Soto, Drake, Cook. Of these
the most symbolic, if not the greatest, was Magellan.

Profiting by the experience of his predecessors, Magellan set out from Spain on September 21, 1519, passed
through the straits that bear his name, then between Pata-
gonia and Terra del Fuego into the Pacific, and then across
to the Philippine Islands, where he died. One of his com-
manders resumed the westward journey, rounded the Cape
of Good Hope, and arrived again in Spain on September
6, 1522.

The world was first circumnavigated in three years. Now
it takes three days. But the effect upon the human imagination was the same as today. Stefan Zweig has recaptured
the contemporary sense of Magellan's achievement:

What sages had suspected for thousands of years, what
learned men had dreamed, was now certain, thanks to the persistent courage of this one man. The earth was round, for a
man had rounded it. . . . The news . . . spread like wildfire
across Europe, rousing immeasurable astonishment and ad-
miration. . . . Other bold discoverers could and would fill in
numerous details in the world-picture, but the basic form of

* Numbered notes are given at the end of the text.

our planet had been ascertained by Magellan, and persists for all time to come. . . . Thirty years had taught more about the place of man's habitation than had thousands and thousands of years before. Though half unwittingly, the generation which had had this intoxicating, this stupendous experience, realized that a new age, the modern age, had begun.[2]

An earth circumnavigated is an unmistakable sphere. A lumberman who lived on the top of one of the lesser Green Mountains said as he gazed out over his landscape, "From here you have the world by the scruff of the neck." Mankind began to have that feeling when the world was first circumnavigated.

And now we do not crawl over the surface of the earth; we swing around it, or if not ourselves, then vicariously as we read the news of the day. We hold it by the scruff of the neck and at arm's length. We take liberties with it. We cross it in every direction, and take new short cuts. We take its picture in new perspectives, as from the polar projection in which the great land masses appear to crowd the Northern Hemisphere. Of these new geographies it has been said, by a writer who reviewed seven of them in one article entitled "The Face of One World," that they "represent the coming of age of the 'global' approach." [3] And even the latest style of artificial globe is no longer attached to a fixed standard, but free to be held in the hand and manipulated at will.

The great age of exploration was also the age in which the foundation of modern science was laid by Galileo and his successors, paving the way for Newton. Modern science is exact science, in which mathematics is wedded to experiment, and in which the theoretical imagination takes the place of observation. Apart from astronomy, its contribution to man's earth-mindedness is less direct and less evident than that of the explorers. But it is to exact science that man owes his growing mastery of the forces of nature and hence his sense of use and possession. As exact science has developed it has demonstrated the unity of nature as one interacting system. It is by exact science and its applications that man has developed those arts of communication and industry which in their turn have brought the ends of the earth together and united its inhabitants in far-flung enterprise and common culture. It is in some degree a condition of all the other forces which have tended to human contact and interdependence.

Man has acquired a progressive familiarity with that spherical earth on which he finds himself, and a progressive experience of grasping and possessing it as a whole. At the same time the human race has come to occupy it more extensively and more densely, so that in reaching out from where he stands to its more distant parts he at the same time establishes contacts with his fellows already domiciled there. There is thus a growing sense of joint and complete terrestrial habitation.

In their wide use of the word *oecumene* (οἰκουμένη) * the Greeks expressed their association of the earth with its human tenants. The oecumene, or inhabited earth, was to the Greeks relative to their own point of origin, but it always signified an enlargement of outlook. It meant the Greek world entire rather than the Athenian or the Spartan world; or the Mediterranean world as distinguished from the merely Greek; or the Mediterranean, Asiatic, and African world as distinguished from the Atlantic; or that part of the surface of the earth which is fit for human habita-

---

* οἰκουμένη, a participial adjective meaning "inhabited," the substantive (earth, country, or land) being understood.

tion—the dry land, for example, as distinguished from the surrounding and uninhabitable ocean. It invited attention to the fringe and outer boundaries of the human world, and in so doing transcended them. The oecumene has steadily enlarged.* It has lost its relativity to Greece or the Mediterranean. Its boundaries have been extended until "oecumenical" now means "world-wide" or "global."

Oecumene was more than a geographical idea. It implied not only human habitation, but other bonds of unity by which the human inhabitants composed a single society. When the Greek city-state was superseded by the Macedonian and Roman empires, oecumene came to mean a world society, composed of many races and provinces, having a common political control, a common law, a common culture, and a common religion, pagan or Christian. Through its sages, seers, and saints this human and terrestrial realm was related to the cosmos as a whole; and the man who was once a citizen of Athens became a citizen of the world and a citizen of the universe.[4] This idea, arising in antiquity, has never been forgotten. The Holy Roman Empire of the Middle Ages, and all later dreams of world federation, are its revivals or lingering echoes.

Meanwhile, however, the boundaries of man's acquaintance with his fellow inhabitants have been extended to the whole earth, and their number has vastly increased.

According to the as yet uncertain and variable results of the modern sciences of geology, archeology, and anthropology, man has inhabited the earth for between six hun-

---

* This is one way of looking at it. According to Professor Werner Wilhelm Jaeger, on the other hand, "The oecumene, the civilized world of 'classical' Greece and Rome, which for two thousand years was believed to be coterminous with the entire earth, has shrunk to a narrow section at its centre."—*Paideia: The Ideals of Greek Culture,* English translation by Gilbert Highet, Oxford University Press, 1939, Vol. I, pp. xiv-xv.

dred thousand and a million years. He dates back at least to the Pleistocene or Glacial period. But, Archbishop Usher and the Book of Genesis to the contrary notwithstanding, it probably took between five hundred and a thousand millions of years to make ready even those uncomfortable accommodations. Measured by cosmic standards, man is a comparatively recent arrival. His origins, whether from one or several stocks, are lowly and his early record unimpressive. But he has possessed an amazing and growing fecundity.

Population figures of the past are notoriously unreliable, and beyond a certain point purely speculative, but there is no doubt of the accelerated increase. Prehistoric men seem usually to have left only single specimens for the edification of future prehistorians. Either that, or their number was extremely small and their existence short and precarious. During the thousands of intervening years we can only infer that the economic conditions of human life were inadequate to support large populations. When we reach the middle of the seventeenth century, we are on firmer ground. According to the estimates of a recent authority, the total population of the earth increased from 545,000,000 in 1650 to over 2,000,000,000 in 1933, the greatest percentage increase having occurred after 1900.

Thus man has taken to heart the Creator's injunction: "Be fruitful, and multiply, and replenish the earth, and subdue it." He has been assisted in doing so by his ever increasing mobility. This is not a matter merely of the ease with which his body can be transported from one locality to another, but also of the ease with which he can adapt himself to different conditions. Science enables men to modify their environment by draining marshes, cutting down forests, irrigating or fertilizing deserts; or they can take their environment with them, as when they heat their houses in cold climates, cool them in hot climates, eradicate diseases, procure a variable food supply, and carry oxygen tanks to high elevations. At the same time, through migration, education, communication, and war, men are becoming less narrowly habituated. Their division into hunters, peasants, herdsmen, fishermen, seafarers, or craftsmen—each such group being bound to its immediate locality by some corresponding manner of livelihood—has become less and less restrictive. Agricultural communities can become industrialized and industrial workers can return to the soil; and the difference between the two types of occupation steadily diminishes.

At the same time that man has become more capable of moving, however, there is less and less room to move into. In view of the great unsettled areas of Africa, Central Asia, and South America, and man's ability to sustain life in all the zones of the earth, whether temperate or intemperate, it would be hasty to predict that there will be no more great migrations; but there can be no doubt of the broad generalization that as in the United States, so on the earth as a whole, the frontier, the wilderness, and even the so-called backward areas are assuming less and less importance. Wherever men go in search of opportunity they are likely to be greeted by the notice "Occupied." Thus despite men's growing versatility, their life on the planet becomes more dense and compact, and they must to an increasing extent create their opportunity where they are rather than seek it elsewhere.

To extend their lives to all parts of the earth men do not need to change their places of residence. They can remain where they are and multiply and lengthen their lines of intercourse. The area of the surface of the earth which a man occupies is proportional to the number and range of his relationships, and not merely to the extent of his travels or the variety of his habitations. He can be said to live in any part of the world with which he exchanges messengers, words, ideas, or goods. He does not need to go if he can send and receive. He does not need to send the messenger if he can send the message. Hence the significance for global unity of the steady and accelerated improvement of the arts of communication.

The beginning of communication is speech, and the role of linguistic learning must not be forgotten merely because it is less spectacular than other human achievements. Without the scholars who have made what is said in any language intelligible in all languages, the world-wide physical facilities of communication would have been useless.

The improvement of the physical instruments of communication is as old and as continuous as the history of man. It comprises the building of roads, bridges, and tunnels; the development of the art of navigation; the substitution of the horse for the human runner, of the horse-drawn vehicle for the human head or back (the horse and buggy was once the symbol of progress!); the displacement of the horse by the automobile; the introduction of steam propulsion on land and sea; the creation of postal systems; the invention of the telegraph and the telephone.

While such changes have been increasingly progressive from the dawn of history, the rate of change has been so accelerated in recent decades as to constitute a revolution rather than an evolution. Of the United States in the ten years prior to the Civil War it has been said that "railroads were spreading over the country like measles in a boarding school." [5] Between 1840 and 1927 the mileage of railways in the United States increased from 2,799 to 249,151. Starting from scratch in 1830, the mileage of the railways of the world reached in 1927 the total of 850,000. These figures take no account of the multiplication of tracks on the same line, or the rapid increase of speed and carrying capacity. Mainly owing to the introduction of steam, the tonnage of the world's mercantile marine increased from 16,600,000 in 1860 to approximately 40,000,000 in 1927.[6] Meanwhile the automobile led to the immense extension and improvement of roads, and the surface of the earth became festooned with wires carrying messages by electrical impulsion; cables were laid beneath the sea.

But these advances, sensational as they were in their day, no longer excite the imagination. We are now, as we say, "air-minded." Messages pass through the air by radio without the aid of wires, and planes without the support of wheels. The speed and the freedom of these new forms of communication have in a few decades surpassed those of their predecessors by intervals formerly compassed in centuries. There is a double sense of rapid change, the change of place and the change of change. The mind as well as the body suffers from a sense of vertigo and breathlessness. And the end is not yet. The impossible has been realized so incessantly that the word "impossible" threatens to become obsolete.

When we say that radio and aviation have "annihilated distance," we mean, of course, that they have reduced the time and trouble required to traverse distance. That the spatial distance remains the same we soon learn when the machine breaks down. In fact the spatial distance then seems, if anything, increased, since as we come to employ more efficient agencies our capacity to employ the old tends to atrophy. We are forgetting how to walk, shout, carry, pay visits, or write letters. But when the machine is working, this time-and-trouble distance is astonishingly reduced. The short-wave radio will carry the human voice to the opposite extremities of the earth in practically no time, and with no trouble at all—which is presumably the limit.

Transport, or the movement of persons and goods from one place to another, still falls far short of being instantaneous. Not even the magic carpet could do that. But with the modern plane proceeding freely through space at only 200 miles per hour, travel time, which was once measured in terms of years, then months, then weeks and days, is now reduced to hours. There is no spot on the surface of the earth more than 60 hours from the local airport. Measured by travel time, the entire earth is now smaller than Washington's United States or Napoleon's Europe.[7] Taking Boston as a center, as is natural to Bostonians, Singapore is as near today as was Pittsburgh in 1790. Since the speed record by air increased from 30 to 440 miles per hour between 1903 and 1938, and is still increasing, it is evident that such calculations convey no adequate picture of the world of tomorrow.

Travel by air, which need no longer take account of the terrain but passes lightly over seas, mountains, polar regions, plays havoc with our preconceived geography. By way of Alaska, it brings us as close to Soviet Russia as is Norway to Scotland. It brings the Caspian Sea, Palestine, and Cairo as near as Buenos Aires. It will be recalled that "a certain lawyer," seeking to tempt Jesus, asked "And who is my neighbour?" If that question were asked today the reply of Jesus would be equally valid; but with the addition, perhaps, of "Who is not?"

Communication by word or travel, or by the transport

of goods, is now so greatly facilitated that a man in one locality can do business with all parts of the earth more easily than was once possible with an adjoining town. This holds of every kind of business, beginning with business proper, or trade and commerce.

The development of economic relations over the surface of the earth exemplifies the extent to which all forms of human enterprise act and react on one another. Trade is dependent on knowledge of distant areas and peoples, on routes of communication, on security and political stability, as well as on specialized techniques and mechanisms such as money, markets, and credit. It is equally true that discovery and improved communications are themselves in large part due to economic motives. It would be folly to attempt any comparative evaluation of these motives. Suffice it to say that the economic motive as distinguished from the rest generates an expansive force of its own.

If men's needs are not satisfied at home, they look abroad. The most rudimentary form of this impulse is the movement from areas of scarcity to areas of abundance. Predatory animal that he is, man goes where he can get what he wants. Tempted by fertility of soil, or mineral wealth, or virgin forests, or game, or water supply, or favorable climate, or open spaces, men press outward from the places where they are born, whether as marauders or as permanent settlers. They take what nature offers, or they take away from their fellows already in possession. In short, given man with his basic appetites, together with the acquired wants which grow with what they feed on, and given natural or artificial objects which will satisfy these appetites and wants, the first will find his way to the second.

Economic activity in the strict sense begins when trade takes the place of plunder. Trade is inherently expansive. Men and groups vary in their specialized capacities, and localities in their specialized resources and products. It is a waste of effort to move the consumer to the goods, or overcome the resistance of their possessors, if the goods will be freely delivered, quid pro quo.* Trade, once inaugurated, tends to become world trade simply by the extension of the same principle. Short of this extension, men continue to look covetously abroad, and resort to plunder if they cannot trade.

The economic unification of the world is strikingly exemplified by the history of Europe. The collapse of the Roman Empire was followed by economic disintegration, despite the survival of the imperial tradition and the cosmopolitanism of learning and religion. This disintegration was the effect of diverse causes—above all, of the deterioration and insecurity of routes of communication, and that multiplication of small political units which is called the feudal system. It is estimated that in the tenth century there were in France alone over 10,000 such feudal manors, each attempting to be economically self-sufficient and preying on whatever commerce came its way. In the fourteenth century the tolls on the Rhine between Bingen and Coblenz amounted to two-thirds of the cost of the delivered goods. This condition was ameliorated in the late Middle Ages by the growth of towns and of the great commercial cities of Germany and Italy. But these raised tariff barriers

---

* The method of moving the consumer to the goods rather than the goods to the consumer is illustrated by feudal practices in Europe about the year 1000. "We read," says a historian, "of the kings and princes being always on the road, traveling with court and retinue from one manor to another, eating up the surplus that had accumulated and then moving on."—Clive Day, *History of Commerce*, 1908, p. 37.

and embargoes against one another and against the surrounding countryside. Even at the end of the sixteenth
century there were fifty toll stations on the Loire between
Orléans and the sea, a distance equal to that between Al-
bany and New York.[8] The bulk of such trade as these
conditions permitted was local—from next to next—distant
trade being confined to a few luxuries.

In the seventeenth and eighteenth centuries the modern
European state superseded manor, town, and city as the
economic unit. This was the period of the so-called mer-
cantilist theory, which encouraged exports and discouraged
imports in order to accumulate money and precious metals
as an instrument of power. Economic relations *within*
states were conceived in terms of mutual benefit, but
economic relations *between* states were conceived in terms
of war. Each state sought to exclude and monopolize, and
to profit at the expense of rival states.

It remained for the nineteenth century, applying the
economic theories of so-called laissez-faire capitalism, and
employing the techniques of the Industrial Revolution, to
develop the possibilities of what we now know as international trade.

Foreign commerce increased literally by "leaps and
bounds." Computed in terms of the dollar value of goods
exchanged, the estimated increase between 1800 and 1900
was from $1,500,000,000 to $20,000,000,000, or at the rate
of over 1200 per cent. This increase was much more rapid
than the increase of population during the same period,
the "share of the average human being in the world's
trade" having grown sixfold.[9] It is to be noted that this
rate of increase occurred in the age of coal and steam,
when the gas engine had been barely invented, before the
Wright brothers had made their first successful flight, and

before the full commercial implications of industrial technology had dawned upon the human mind.

Before and after the First World War the curve of foreign commerce still pointed upward. The decline after 1930 can be attributed to world depression and impending war, and to the artificial restrictions to which these gave rise. The economic forces themselves have made for a steady growth of trade, foreign and domestic. The transport plane and the automotive truck have been added to the steamship and the railroad. To the old incentives of trade have been added the requirements of modernized industry. Manufacturing employs an ever increasing variety of raw materials, drawn to various centers from all parts of the earth. Mass production requires world markets, and a returning flow of goods from distant consumers. Thus a low-priced American automobile contains 185 or more different materials brought largely from abroad; its manufacture is profitable only when it is produced in numbers which far exceed local or even national consumption; it can be sent abroad only because the country is prepared to import other goods to a like amount.[10]

Trade thus creates two-way channels, girdling the globe and reaching into all its remotest corners, and along which there is a perpetual flow of goods. The effect of this single circulatory system is to develop a sameness of material goods, designed to meet the same basic human needs, drawn from the same terrestrial resources, and produced by the same industrial techniques.

The development of economic life, together with increased knowledge of the surface of the earth, the increased density of population, and the improvement of the arts of communication, has tended to bind mankind together as the tenants of the common earth. What shall be said of man's political allegiance?

The answer to that question is perhaps hanging in the balance at the present time. Politics both unites men and divides them, and an excess of either unity or division has tended to generate the opposite. The earlier empires of antiquity—Egyptian, Assyrian, Babylonian, Persian—were the outcome of the lust for wealth and dominion. The Hellenic empires and the Roman empires, pagan and Holy, embodied the idea of a world community in which cultural and religious unity were combined with unified political control. Great empires fell apart, through insurrection at the bottom, decay at the top, or attack from without. From the ruins of feudalism, tribalism, or other forms of political separatism arose the nation-state, based on the maxim of strength through union. But this strength was measured by rivalry abroad as well as by order and prosperity within, and gave rise to divisions whose conflicts were more deadly because their units were larger. It seemed only to have substituted a few great barriers and enmities for the many small ones. Furthermore, in proportion as nationality came to be associated with self-government and expressed a demand for cultural self-expression, it tended to breed a new multiplicity of its own.

At the dawn of the present century, then, the world was divided politically into many nation-states, and other groups—minorities, colonies, or dependencies—aspiring to become nation-states. The tensions, frustrations, and destructive conflicts bred by this situation pointed to one or the other of two alternatives—either a new type of empire, in which one state should impose its national will on all the rest, or *inter*nationalism. Neither alternative has been achieved, but that the world is today, as never before, alive to the vital significance of world-wide political relations is incontestable. Foreign policy and domestic policy can no longer be sharply separated; the political problems on which a citizen is obliged to form an opinion are now of global range and complexity. However one views the matter, whether in terms of power, or bare self-preservation, or peace, or national self-interest, or the good of mankind at large, political isolationism is outmoded. All predictions and proposals for the future—whether a world-state imposed by conquest or erected by agreement, a federation of nations, a system of spheres of influence, or a network of alliances—all are now based on the assumption that the world is politically interdependent, and that its division into different political entities each ignoring the rest, or treating them as enemies, is no longer possible.

At the same time that man's common earthly habitat has been disclosed to him by science and its inhabitants have been linked together by contact and interaction, man has come, on the whole and despite influences to the contrary, to be increasingly aware of his community of kind. This is in part a sense of the common lot and mutual interdependence of earth dwellers. But it goes beyond this to a recognition of kinship.

In discovering one another men have been made newly aware of their great diversity. The stranger has been visited, and observed in all his strangeness. The earlier sense of human sameness resting on limited acquaintance, or on the distant perspectives of religion and metaphysics, was contradicted by the discovery of primitive races scarcely recognizable as human, and of alien societies astonishingly different in their customs and beliefs. But the recognition of kinship has survived this shock, and has emerged stronger than ever because now it is armed against disillusionment. In these days it takes a large understanding, a broad tolerance, and even a strong stomach to admit all men to the family circle, but never before have men been so willing, or so obliged, to do so. Lazarus takes his place at the table. The very boldness and brutality of its enemies have aroused the friends of humanity to its defense.

Man is conscious, as never before, of common roots and common destiny, or common limitations and common potentialities. Even the recognition of their lowly biological origin and their ineradicable taint of selfishness and unreason has served, like the idea of original sin, to bind men together. The discovery of different folkways has only served to emphasize the common underlying needs and appetites, and the common arts required for their satisfaction. And despite the awareness of many forms of religious faith, and of rival and incommensurable ideologies, never has there been a clearer recognition of the universality of civilization, based on a common standard of living and on the common principles of dignity, freedom, justice, compassion, and self-development. This sense of kinship has been not only strengthened by its overcoming of new doubts and its assimilation of new facts, but has been extended by mutual acquaintance, until for the first time men in the flesh begin to correspond to the abstract idea of mankind.

An adequate picture of growing world unity must take account not only of the wide range of relationships but also of the extent to which they reach the lives and minds of the masses of mankind. Railroads or air routes bind the world together not only by the length of trunk lines but by the ramification of their lateral lines. Rural free delivery is not less important than international postal service. The unifying effect of the telegraph and the telephone depends on the wide distribution of local stations. The radio integrates the world because so many human beings possess and use radio sets. The press performs a similar function because of the large circulation of urban newspapers and because the great press services carry the events of the world to country newspapers. The growth of economic interdependence is a function not only of the distance and volume of foreign trade, but also of the degree to which imported commodities enter into the daily uses of the general consumer. Thus to appreciate the extent to which many scattered localities are becoming one world it is necessary to multiply the maximum range of each relationship by its local diffusion.

Hence the importance of popular education which enables a rapidly mounting proportion of mankind to read, hear, and speak with understanding. In an illiterate world the technical arts of communication would convey their messages to nobody, or only to a thin top crust. Hence the importance of a rising standard of living, enabling ever increasing numbers of mankind to possess and use the improved instruments of publicity, as well as the products of a world economy. These factors of distribution bring the whole wide earth home to its humblest human inhabitants, and create in the mind of every man a more and more lively sense of the terrestrial community.

The difference between the near and the remote will never be obliterated, and the greater part of a man's life will always be lived in that local neighborhood of space and time and social intimacy into which he has been born.

Each man's life will always have its own peculiar center. But there is no doubt that its circumference has been greatly widened, and that it tends to a constantly increasing extent to coincide with the circumference of the globe. A man's mind and his deeds reach out to the extremities of the earth, and these extremities are brought to him where he is. The visible horizon is no longer a limit, but a passage and an invitation. All the major events in human life become daily news before they have time to become history, and more and more men feel a greater and greater compulsion to do something about them, even if it be only to grasp and assimilate. The world abroad is woven more and more closely in the texture of more and more of the world at home.

It would be premature for men to congratulate themselves upon this increasing unity. At the present moment men are suffering rather than profiting from it. While it facilitates transactions and creates new opportunities, it also makes men more vulnerable to attack, and raises new problems.

The simplest solution of human problems is by ignorance. The next simplest solution of human problems is to evade them. In the past distance has been a refuge as well as an obstacle. If human relations became intolerable, it was once possible to run away, and become inaccessible. Accessibility is a two-way passage. If it is convenient to be able to reach others, the reverse is often highly inconvenient. The roominess and spaciousness of earth was one of its unearned and most prized blessings.

There was a security in isolation, and that security is now lost. There was also an ease and an economy in isolation. Provincialism is narrow, but it is snug and comfortable. Men are expected to do what they can, and when the possibilities are widened, the expectation is correspondingly increased. If a man can be aware of the whole earth, and of all mankind, and can act at global distances, he feels obliged to do so. Every form of human life thus grows more complicated, requires more thought and imagination, and the mastery of larger and more intricate chains of relationship. Now that more can be done and done more quickly, time is more valuable, and leisure, measured by what one *might* do, becomes more costly.

Men can by taking thought increase the size of their instruments and mechanisms. In times of expansion they can create new agencies, or new departments of old agencies, to take care of new business. They can build Pentagon Buildings for additional office space. But it is still impossible for man by taking thought to add a cubit to his stature. He cannot enlarge his brain and develop a new set of lobes to take care of his international interests and affairs. The capacity of his cranium remains the same, and as it becomes more and more crowded and noisy he suffers to an increasing extent what are aptly called "headaches."

If in a certain specific and restricted sense the world is growing smaller, it is equally true, and more significant, to say that the world in which each man lives is growing greater, and its problems graver. Problems once solved or escaped by remoteness and unawareness have now to be faced and solved by the creation of new human institutions. Men live in a greater world, embracing the whole of earth and all its inhabitants, and their lives must be organized in the same proportions. The principles and methods by which men can hope to live safely and well in this greater world will be set forth in the chapters that follow.

CHAPTER TWO

Moral Foundations of World Order

THAT "one world" which can be said already to exist, and to have developed at an accelerated pace during recent decades, is not a just and happy world. It would be more accurate to say that the increase of contact and interdependence has created a growing need of moral unity. When we say that "isolationism" is now obsolete, we mean, in the first place, that there is a network of relationships which connects man with man throughout the globe; or that man's field of action, in which he gives and receives, now embraces all men of whatever nation, race, condition, or locality. But we also mean, in the second place, that human problems which could once be solved on a lesser scale must now be solved on a global scale. We mean that human problems which were once soluble by separation must now be solved by organization; and that the fruitfulness of co-operation, which was once limited to the relations of individuals or groups within a single society, can now be extended to the relations between societies. World unity in this second or moral sense is not an accomplished fact of which account is to be taken, but a plan to be executed—an imperative necessity and an inviting opportunity, but a task of immense difficulty. Mankind has achieved what Pope Pius XII has called a "unity of dwelling place." [1] How to live there in peace and abundance has yet to be learned.

The unity of the world is not necessarily a good thing, despite the favorable overtones of the blessed word "unity." It is curious that men should have been disposed to accept this idea in general when it is so painfully contrary to their experiences in particular. Rubbing elbows produces friction. The poet is not the only man who feels that "The world is too much with us." There is, for example, the householder whose next idea after installing a telephone is to have somebody else answer it for him and say that he is in conference or not at home. There is the hapless islander, visited by conquerors, salesmen, or missionaries from abroad.

People often have the best of reasons for wishing to be let alone, for excluding, as well as including, relations with their fellow men. Unity is not all love and fellowship and order; unity is also intrusion, interference, jealousy, confusion, and hate. "In that day, saith the Lord of hosts, shall ye call every man his neighbour under the vine and under the fig tree." But neighbors can be bad neighbors; a neighborhood is not the same thing as a Good Neighbor Policy. "Now," says a recent writer, "when a given country or nation" is "member of a large family of nations comprising a now much shrunken and steadily shrinking world so that its members are living huddled closely together, 'cheek by jowl,' each looking into the other's back yard, approving some of the conditions seen there, disapproving and being irritated by other things, envying still others," we are compelled to intervene in one another's hitherto private affairs.[2] Domestic life becomes a matter of public concern. Nor is the intimacy of domestic life itself a solvent of the problems of human relations. The idea that the human race is becoming one great big family may well be regarded with apprehension, if not with dismay. It is not clear that the way to get on with one's relatives is to live with them under one roof. Sometimes we have good reasons for believing that the less we see of them, the better.

We catch diseases from our neighbors and our families. At a recent meeting of the American Public Health Association, Raymond D. Fosdick presented one of the aspects of world unity as follows:

Whether it is malaria or cholera or plague or tuberculosis or whatever the disease may be, the nations of the world face these enemies of mankind not as isolated groups behind boundary lines but as members of the human race projected suddenly into a frightening propinquity. We did not plan it this way, and science did not plan it this way. We wandered unwittingly into this situation. But here we are—all nations and races jammed together into a single community, tied together by bonds which cannot now be severed. It is indeed one world—one future—one destiny.[3]

It is to be noted that Mr. Fosdick speaks of "frightening propinquity." Elsewhere in the same address he made it clear that this new propinquity does not solve the problem of public health, but creates it on a world scale. Public health can no longer be dealt with by the simple method of quarantine. The only remedy is to stamp out disease in whatever part of the world it occurs.

All the technological developments by which the world is knit more closely together increase the danger and destructiveness of evil forces. When any part of the world is "afire, we all get burned." Insults are as promptly and widely communicated as messages of love; technology recognizes no difference. It is possible to lie as well as to speak the truth by telephone, telegraph, or radio; wires and waves do not discriminate. One can be cruel or kind by any technical art, however improved. It is true that there need be no more helplessness, since help is now easily and quickly available; but hurtfulness is transmitted no less swiftly and abundantly than helpfulness. One can murder or steal by automobile or airplane more easily and more effectively than by horse and buggy. The same techniques are as useful to the criminal as to the police.

Armies are transported by the same means as friendly missions. Modern methods of communication and transport have increased the menace of hostility, and have spread it abroad to all corners of the earth. The latest techniques of propulsion carry messengers of death across thousands of miles. Missiles have increased in range and destructiveness from the arrow and the bullet to the blockbuster and atomic bomb, and to the ten-ton projectile, which, it is now confidently predicted, can someday be hurled by a rocket from the coast of Europe to New York. The same skill and invention that heals wounds is used to inflict them. Mass production and the industrial arts have found their most impressive demonstration in the total mobilization for war. Every application of science that has drawn parts of the earth together has increased the power of a ruthless and scheming nation to take advantage of the unwary and to plunge all mankind into devastating war. No longer can societies ensure their safety by withdrawing to a distance, or by retiring behind natural barriers of sea or mountains, or by creating uninhabited marches between their boundaries.

The one incontrovertible fact is that men must in a

new and radical sense learn to live together if they are not to die together. They cannot escape one another. Their togetherness cannot be undone, but must be rendered beneficent. The unity of the world already achieved by technology sets the problem but does not solve it; it provides means, but no assurance that these will be used for good ends. The world is dense and interacting, but it is still divided. If by "one world" is meant a world of harmony, agreement, and partnership, it will not be achieved merely by giving free play to the forces which have increased the world's density and interaction. The conquest of space and time is a fruitless victory unless it is accompanied by a conquest of evil.

The present unity of the world adds strength to the forces of evil, and can, if men will, but only if they will, add greater strength to the forces of good. Thus far it has served only to arouse men from their complacency and to sharpen the grim alternatives with which they are faced. Men may use their new powers to destroy one another, or to destroy all save one exhausted and debased survivor. Or they may use their new powers constructively, and out of their injuries and fears create a world in which all shall survive and live more abundantly.

The crowning unity of the world, by which its existing unity of contact and interaction is made good, is properly described as a *moral* unity. We are undertaking to create "a new order founded on moral principles." [4] An explanation of the term "moral" is now in order. There is an inclination to avoid the use of moral terms, and to prefer some more profane vocabulary. But this prejudice is the result of failing to understand what morality is. We are accustomed to think of it in terms of prohibitions or stereotyped maxims, usually identified with the commands of a superior being, whether God, ruler, parent, or that inner sanction called conscience. This conception of morality is largely responsible for the false antithesis between the stern morality of duty and the beneficent counsels of utility and happiness.

The essence of morality can best be understood by stating the situation out of which it arises and for which it provides a remedy. Whatever may be true of angelic beings, the interests of men and animals, living in the same space-time world, tend to collide. What one interest demands can often be obtained only at the expense of another interest. Two hungers cannot both consume the same bread, but they can want the same bread and endeavor to possess it. When two animals or men are aware of this conflict of interest, they will endeavor to exclude or dispossess one another. Their hunger is then converted into enmity, and they devote to one another's destruction the energy which was originally directed to the obtaining of food. One or both will then go hungry, and perhaps perish. Nature has equipped animals and men for this deadly struggle—endowing them with predatory and combative instincts, and with physiological mechanisms, such as the adrenal glands, with which to augment their force and endurance.

This reign of the tooth and the claw appears to be the design of nature below a certain level of biological development. Man springs from that level, and can revert to it. But with man there appears another design represented by his so-called higher faculties. Sympathy and fellow feeling develop as a check on his combative instincts. Social institutions provide a rational and moral solution of conflict in place of violence. His reason sees the possibility of avoiding collision by rerouting and organizing his interests. Recognizing the folly of mutual negation, he sets himself the task of devising a mode of life by which his energies can flow into positive and constructive channels. By organization he not only averts the destructiveness of conflict, but earns the dividend of collective action, since the result of combined effort is greater than the sum of the results of isolated efforts.

This is morality in the basic sense—nonconflict and co-operation achieved by organization, because of the hurt which they avoid and the help which they yield. Morality does not consist essentially in hewing to a line of precept or command, but in doing good. The standard virtues and maxims all present or accentuate some facet of this solid meaning: benevolence, the will to do good; justice, the apportionment of good; prudence and temperance, the subordination of lesser to greater good; courage, the strength of goodwill in the presence of obstacles and dangers; the Golden Rule, the recognition of another's good as though it were one's own; happiness, the enjoyment of good.

Moralists are afraid to refer to happiness, unless by some more high-sounding word such as "felicity," "blessedness," or "well-being." The word owes its moral disrepute to the fact that it suggests selfish happiness as distinguished from the happiness of others, and low happiness as distinguished from high. If happiness means the getting of what is desired and the having of what is liked, for all men and on every level of activity, then this is what is meant by good in the final and irreducible sense of that term. There is no right, no freedom, no duty, no obligation, that does not conduce directly or indirectly to the happiness of sentient beings.

Morality requires *the subordination of partial to total good*. The good of morality is individual; but because it embraces *all* individuals, it sets limits to *each* individual. Hence the negative or forbidding side of morality. It is a part of morality that the happiness of one individual should be consistent with that of other individuals. Morality denies the one only in order that it may affirm the many.

Human life is arranged in concentric circles of lesser and greater radius. Morality speaks for the wider and overrules the narrower. It sets the total person above any one of his appetites; the family or neighborhood above any of its particular persons; the nation above the neighborhood; and the aggregate of all nations above anyone or any group less than all.

Morality, speaking always for the wider circle, has different organs of expression. It may be voiced by the scruples of the narrower circle, which restrain its selfishness. It may be voiced by the feeling of humanity which, although it springs from a single person or group, is directed to every other person or group, without limit. It may be voiced by the public sentiment and opinion of the wider circle, shaming the narrower into compliance. It may be voiced by the excluded persons or groups, who believe that they do not receive their due share of good. It may be voiced by the great social institutions whose purpose it is to organize the wider circle for the good of all its members. Or it may be voiced by those who speak in the name of God as one who wills the good of all creatures.

The moral unity of the world consists of the extension of this same morality—the same standards, precepts, and institutions—to the interrelation of nations and of all mankind, so that they may live and let live, and work together in order that all may live more abundantly.

Morality, inserted at the point where one human interest touches another, converts their rivalry from hurtfulness into helpfulness, and thus conduces to that maximum happiness of each man which is consistent with the maximum happiness of all men. It is one of the tragic paradoxes of human life that the institutions which men create for the sake of their happiness become separated from this end. It is quite evident that an economy exists for the happiness of the consumer, and that production and distribution are means to that end; but as economy grows more and more complicated, the poor consumer who is its only excuse for being is forgotten, or is considered as a means of production. Government exists not for its own sake, but for the sake of the governed, whose interests the government is designed to promote. Law exists for the freedom and security enjoyed by those who live under law, and not for the sake of legality itself, or for the benefit of the lawyer. Similarly, in art technique or learning tends to take the place of aesthetic enjoyment; in religion clericalism or ecclesiasticism gets in the way of piety; and in education it is often necessary to remind teachers and administrators that the school exists for the benefit of the scholar. Morality is the friend of the ultimate consumer all along the line, and of all the consumers—the *people* whose happiness is the ultimate criterion by which all human institutions should be judged—the people who suffer and enjoy, the people who in a mechanized, organized, and specialized world are so easily but unforgivably forgotten.

"It is axiomatic," writes Sumner Welles, "that the foreign policy of the United States, like that of any other nation, should be based on enlightened selfishness." [5] This proposition is not axiomatic. The first requirement of an axiom is that its meaning should be clear. But what is meant by the word "should"? Does it mean what morally ought to be? Does the proposition mean that morality and selfishness are the same thing? Or does it mean that nations, unlike persons, are exempt from moral obligations? Or does it mean that selfishness ought to be enlightened? Or does it mean that a selfishness which is enlightened ceases to be selfish? Or does it mean that the best means of promoting the unselfish good of all nations is to assign to each nation the task of looking out exclusively for itself? No one of these statements is true; nor does the author adhere consistently to any one of these statements in the remainder of his admirable book.

The wide acceptance of the standard of enlightened selfishness is due to its seeming to ask nothing. It appeals to the line of least resistance. A man wants something, and sets out to get it; that is his selfishness. He adopts means of getting it; and his enlightenment consists in the degree to which his relation of means to end coincides with the relation of cause and effect.

But there are other men with their wants, and there is morality, which recognizes the wants of all men. What is the answer? One answer is that the way for any man to get what he himself wants is precisely the same as the way for all men to satisfy *all* wants. If this were so, then it would be easy to persuade a man to be just and humane, since justice and humanity would then demand only a more successful pursuit of what he already wants. He could make his terms with morality once and for all—and thereafter forget it. His selfishness would receive the endorsement of conscience. Having paid a nominal initiation fee, he would become a life member of moral society with all further dues remitted.

It is not surprising that this painless morality is much in demand. But unhappily it is both false and dangerous. It is false because the way of morality and the way of selfishness are *not* the same. The way of satisfying one man's wants is not the same as the way of satisfying his wants together with those of his neighbor. What a man will do in pursuit of his own interests regardless of others differs from what he will do if he shares the concern which others feel for their interests. This is sometimes expressed by saying that the right act is that which is approved by the disinterested spectator, where "disinterested" means all-interested—as the disinterested judge represents the interests of both parties to a dispute, or the government the interests of all members and sections of society, or God the interests of all mankind. Morality does not coincide with selfishness, or reinforce it by providing more enlightened means; it sets limits to selfishness. The broader supersedes the narrower view; the voice of morality, speaking for the whole, checks the promptings of selfishness, speaking for a limited part.

The following example will clarify the difference between self-interest and morality. In February 1944, the United States negotiated a treaty with Mexico over the division of the waters of the Colorado, Rio Grande, and Tijuana rivers. The ratification of the treaty on April 18, 1945, was a triumph of justice, or approximate justice, over the all too enlightened self-interest of certain persons living in California.[6] The Colorado River rises in Wyoming, and flows through or between Arizona, Colorado, Nevada, New Mexico, Texas, and Utah, as well as Wyoming. During the last 50 miles of its course it flows through Mexico, and finally into the Gulf of California. Two nations, seven states, hundreds of towns, and thousands of individuals were interested in what had been done, and what was going to be done, to this river. Among these individuals were certain big California farmers who can always use more water, and others who are in the water business—the less water the Mexicans have of their own, the more these Californians can sell to them. Mexico, on the other hand, is an arid country which greatly needs water for irrigation and to increase its food supply. The treaty divides the total annual flow of the river among the interested parties. It is described as "fair," as "hardly generous," and as giving Mexico even less than it would receive from an impartial tribunal.

If we return to the selfishly interested parties in California, it is clear that the treaty does not give them as much water as they would have obtained by ignoring Mexican interests, or as much as they could profitably use if they had it. They knew this, and they were enlightened about it—enlightened enough, it is alleged, to spend considerable funds for the purpose of converting public opinion and public officials to their private view of the matter. It was impossible to persuade them that it is to their *personal profit* to be generous, or even fair to Mexico, or even to the rest of California and the United States. And from their point of view they were quite right. If the treaty succeeds, it will not be because it is the most enlightened way of serving their selfishness, but because there were enough people having political influence or authority who took the larger view of the matter and overruled their selfishness.

To equate morality with enlightened selfishness is dangerous as well as false. It is dangerous because it is partially true. Selfishness does dictate a consideration of others up to a certain point—in order to attract customers, or conciliate opponents, or make allies. But it is equally true that beyond a certain point the way of selfishness and the way of morality diverge. Enlightened selfishness knows how to locate that point—the point at which the interests of others will cease to serve one's own and become a nuisance to be abated, or an obstacle to be removed from the path. Nazi Germany knew how to implement its selfishness with concessions and fair promises—when to bribe, and when to destroy.

Those who equate morality and selfishness must be prepared to show that a Nazi Germany could have obtained what it wanted—racial priority, territorial conquest, or slave labor—by giving the Jews, the Czechs, and the Poles what *they* wanted; or by seeking the good of all men, whether Aryan or non-Aryan, German or non-German. Nazi selfishness was too enlightened to suppose anything so absurd. The Nazi leaders knew that they could have their way only at the expense of others, and they were not mistaken. A greater enlightenment would not have altered that fact, but only the preparation, the timing, and the strategy of their aggression. As it was, and despite their failure, they understood their business well, and were more enlightened in the pursuit of their selfishness than were their appeasing victims in the pursuit of theirs; more enlightened, until it was almost too late, than the outraged conscience of mankind.

The false equation between morality and enlightened selfishness is dangerous because it evades the moral problem, which is to change men's wills and not their calculations, their hearts and not their heads, their ends and not their means. It is dangerous because it makes promises which cannot be fulfilled. A morality which promises all things to all men must fail to deliver, and will be discredited by its bankruptcy, as the reckless demagogue is discredited after he takes office. By allowing selfishness to borrow its clothes, morality exalts its one irreconcilable and deadly enemy; namely, immorality. For morality is precisely the overcoming of selfishness.

If by selfishness is meant a man's pursuit of the interests which he calls his own, regardless of what these interests are, and taking account of the interests of other men only insofar as they serve his own; and if by enlightenment is meant the knowledge which best serves this selfishness— then no amount of enlightenment will square this self-ishness with the general good. Sometimes, however, "en-lightened self-interest" is taken to mean something very different.

There are many kinds of selves. There is, for example, the self of the professional soldier. It would not do to promise him preferment and prestige in a reign of peace. Or there is the patrician, whose vocation is rank and privi-lege. It would scarcely be enlightened of him to join forces with the advocates of social equality. There is a sensual, greedy, power-loving, arrogant kind of self; and there is a rational, temperate, merciful, and generous kind of self. How far a man's self-interest coincides with morality may then be said to depend on the kind of self he has, or is. We can say that the self-interest of a rational, temperate, mer-ciful, and generous man coincides with morality. But that is only because we have already put the morality into the self. The self-interest of a moral self coincides with the happiness of mankind, but only because that is what is meant by a moral self. The moral point is the interest of the man in mankind, and provided his interest is so di-rected, how much he thinks of it as his own is unimportant.

To some the adjective "enlightened" when attached to self-interest signifies the moral self. There are the possibilities of a moral self in every man. He has a faculty of reason which prompts him to disinterestedness, and faculties of sympathy and imagination by which he identifies himself with the interests of others. A man in whom these faculties do not play their full part falls short of being a man. The happiness which springs from the exercise of these faculties may be described as a peculiarly human happiness. It relates morality to human nature, so that it becomes a form of self-regulation and not an alien tyranny. It justifies that claim of the human person to be considered as an end in himself, and never as a means only, of which Kant spoke. It confers on man that dignity of which we hear so much today—that dignity, not merely titular, which is man's by virtue of what he has it in him to be.

But this ideal of complete manhood should not be allowed to obscure the fact that actual human persons are rarely complete, and are only occasionally ruled by their higher faculties. This being the fact, it will not do to entrust the cause of morality to the existing wills of unregenerate men, least of all when they are shrewd and calculating. It will not do to promise men that morality will give them that on which they have presently set their hearts. That reign of peace, justice, and humanity which is the moral goal will give to each man only his fair share of its total benefits. Such a world will not please or serve the hard, acquisitive, and domineering man whose satisfaction is enhanced by its cost to others, but only the man who prefers a happiness which is shared by others, who prefers love to hate, truth to lies, and a general atmosphere of mutual goodwill to one of suspicion and hostility.

The one world of which we fondly dream is not designed to satisfy the exclusive interest of any man or any group. It contains no masters' or servants' quarters. It serves each interest only by serving all interests. It rests on this widest and all-inclusive base, and on nothing less.

It is not an idle dream. It is not a mere playful exercise of the imagination, but a project to which men are driven by practical necessity. It is not an impossible goal, but lies within the range of human faculties at their highest and best.

Though not an idle dream, it is nonetheless an exciting dream. It is not a least of evils but a maximum of good. It stirs the enthusiasm of earnest souls, and the ridicule of those who would excuse their moral indolence. Professor Carl Becker says of the Abbé de Saint-Pierre that he was described as the man "at whom everyone laughs, and who is alone serious." And Becker adds: "Well, let us join the others and laugh at the Abbé. . . . Let us laugh at him, by all means, but be well assured that when we do we are laughing at the eighteenth century, at its preoccupation with human welfare, at its *penchant* for projects." [7]

The Abbé wrote a book, which was edited by his friend Rousseau, and which bore the title of *Project for Perpetual Peace*. It contains these words:

No grander, more admirable, or more useful project has occupied the human mind than that of a perpetual and universal peace among all the European peoples; and no author has better merited the attention of the public than he who advances means of carrying this project into effect. Indeed such an affair is not likely to leave a sensitive and virtuous man without some modicum of enthusiasm; and perhaps the illusion of a truly humane heart, whose zeal makes all things appear easy, is to be preferred to that harsh and negative intellect which always finds in its own indifference the first obstacle to everything which can promote the public good.[8]

The Abbé's dream looked no further than to the peace of Europe; that world-wide peace of which others have dreamed and of which we dream today merits enthusiasm even more intoxicating, commingled with a correspondingly greater sobriety in the examination of the means by which the dream may be made to come true. The general specifications are known, the materials are at hand; there remains the laborious toil of building.

That which has to be built is a system of institutions which shall not only embrace the whole surface of the earth but also represent every human interest. It need not, and should not, absorb these interests, but directly or indirectly it must affect them all and make room for them all. The vast complexity of the project must not blind us to the singleness of its moral purpose. That great man Winston Churchill, who is sometimes as greatly wrong as he is usually greatly right, and the aptness of whose words is equaled only by their occasional ineptness, delivered himself as follows: "This is not a time for ideological preferences for one side or the other, and certainly we, His Majesty's Government, have not indulged ourselves in this way at all." [9]

Mr. Churchill's statement was false to the professions of his Allies, and did injustice to His Majesty's Government. For whether or not it be named an "ideology," the present united effort of the United Nations is founded on a common creed—that is, a common idea imperfectly translated into a common purpose by a union of wills. If the Prime Minister refused to call it an ideology, it is perhaps because to him it is too self-evident and instinctive to deserve the name. But in the official declarations and agreements of their statesmen and in the testimony of thousands upon thousands of their private citizens, the United Nations have linked this war not only to a common danger but to a common cause, describable only in the well-worn terms of the moral vocabulary:

> Gentleness, Virtue, Wisdom, and Endurance—
> These are the seals of that most firm assurance
> Which bars the pit over Destruction's strength . . .
> These are the spells by which to reassume
> An Empire o'er the disentangled doom.[10]

These are the terms of that moral piety which is reaffirmed by the Allied powers against its defiant rejection by the impudent and shameless anti-morality of the enemy. It "bars the pit over Destruction's strength" by the greater strength of the moral will. It envisions a "just and durable peace" which deserves to be durable because it is just. It is to this ancient and eternally valid creed that we look for a fresh solution of newly grave and difficult problems; it is by this creed that we seek to convert that one world which is a fact, for better or worse, into the one world which ought to be: choosing the better, and rejecting the worse. It is by this creed that we hope to untie the tangled Gordian knots that can no longer be cut by isolationism. It is by the renewed vigor and intelligent application of this creed that we hope to overcome the time lag that now separates our still world-breaking social institutions from an already world-making technology.

There are many ways of working for the one cause; and there are many ways of applying its identical morality.[11] There is a division of labor by which, while all are moral partners, each may follow his own aptitude and speak his own preferred language. Those who are political-minded hope to reconcile the conflict of states or of national interests which otherwise break into violence. They seek to control the aggressor by the collective will of all. They may for good and sufficient reasons reject the idea of a world-state, but at the very least they hope by solemn multilateral agreement to achieve an over-all direction of human affairs and a world-wide civil order analogous to that achieved in particular societies that live under government. Lawyers and students of jurisprudence hope to develop a body of rules by which the rights of nations shall be safeguarded and by which the behavior of nations in relation to one another shall be predictable. They hope to bring such rules into force and to provide a court by which they shall be authoritatively interpreted and developed.

Businessmen and economists hope by international agreement and a more international outlook to mitigate the rivalries, and remove the suspicions and barriers which prevent the fullest utilization of the earth's physical resources and of man's powers of invention and industrial organization; to the end that material goods may be more abundantly available to each and to all, and "to each" consistently with "to all."

To scientists, artists, and men of letters, to students and lovers of folkways, the world's better unity signifies the preservation of indigenous cultures, the cross-fertilization of national cultures, and the reconciliation of the universal values of knowledge and taste with those warmer and more colorful manifestations which express the individuality and the native genius of particular historic societies. Those engaged in education—teachers and students, journalists and publicists—are, in their several ways, interested in the nourishment and the forming of the human mind. They insist that if men are to live happily and fruitfully in one world, they must know about it, and must acquire dispositions that accord with its peculiar global requirements. And, finally, the religious leaders and the great body of sincere and ardent believers look to their faith, or to the teachings and prophetic utterances of sacred books. They find the key to the salvation of all men where they find the salvation of one—in God's universal love, or man's cosmic destiny, or the essential meaning of life.

Thus the exponents of politics, law, economics, culture, education, and religion, though they speak with different accents, speak one common moral language; speaking of universality, of order, harmony, and co-operation, of world-wide well-being and human development, of love and justice. They may also learn from one another, borrowing the means to their ends, or the ends which give meaning and unity to their means. They are moral allies, or if rivals, then rivals in well-doing.

The common moral cause is perpetually lost to view amidst the bewildering confusion of the total enterprise, or because of preoccupation with immediate necessities. It was sharply dramatized by the Nazi enemy's bold avowal of its opposite, and suffused with indignation by his brutalities. But lines grow less sharp and the feelings less poignant. There are always those moral renegades whose power to scandalize or appeal to selfishness and inertia procures them a wide acceptance.

To keep the central moral issue alive and clear is everybody's business. War is everybody's fault and peace is everybody's business. There are those who argue that the causes of war are political or legal; there is another and formidable party which argues that its causes are economic; and others which would fix the ultimate responsibility upon culture, education, or religion.[12] There is no single cause of the disease, nor any single remedy. The present world's disorder is everybody's responsibility, and to transform it into beneficent order is everybody's duty and everybody's hope.

The following paragraph has recently appeared in a vigorous letter contributed to the *Boston Herald:*

Dramatic, eye-opening appeals and statements of fact must be repeatedly made to awaken the sometimes all-too-placid American electorate to the cunning, creeping, insidious miasma of putrid idealism which, like termites, is eating away at the structural foundations of this nation.[13]

Equally unfragrant gas bombs are from time to time hurled into the camp of the realists. This war of epithets —"visionary," "crackpot," "pipe dream," "compromise," "opportunist," "reactionary"—though it has its comic side, must not be taken too lightly. It creates antagonistic parties out of two halves of the same morality. It has all the paralyzing effect of a civil war.

Ideals are not mere rosy pictures created by the imagination, or fairy tales composed for children. They are goals to be achieved by human flesh and blood and embodied in a firm structure of physical and social organization. In other words, an ideal is something to realize. Having an ideal implies that it be translated into concrete results—that is what it means to *have* it. The loftier the ideal, the more the facts that have to be taken into account, and the longer and more involved the chains of cause and effect that have to be understood. If by an idealist is meant a man who not only imagines ideals but pursues them, then the more idealistic he is, the more soberly and patiently will he respect the instruments and the circumstances on which his success depends. In other words, the more idealistic, the more realistic.

Or let us take it the other way round. Reality is not something to be passively accepted. Reality is there in order that something may be done about it: the soil to be cultivated, the forces of nature to be harnessed to man's uses, and the ever present weaknesses and destructive impulses of human nature to be overcome. The battle is not only for survival, but for the building and protection of what we call civilization. The battle is not a real battle, and its victories have no meaning, unless we suppose that it has a purpose beyond a mere struggle for power. There are remoter goals, and there are intermediate goals which must be attained and left behind on the way. The realist will be one whose map, compass, and general plan, frequently consulted, embrace the remoter goals; so that every movement, even though it should be a temporary retreat or detour, will be a phase of forward movement. The realist will adapt his action to the terrain and to the strength or maneuvers of the enemy, but he will also look ahead to the distant future—his feet on the ground, but his eyes in the front of his head. In other words, the more realistic, the more idealistic.

It is this combination of alertness and vision, dealing with the here and now, but oriented by the wider and longer view, which is required for all great human efforts, such as that in which mankind is now engaged. Morality is the realization of an ideal. A true realism and a true idealism thus fit together as complementary parts of one whole. There is a false realism and a false idealism when one is made to do the work of both. The false realism takes the real as the ideal. The false idealism takes the ideal as the real. The one perceives facts, and the other contemplates images. Both are stationary and self-satisfied. The one has no standard by which to measure attainment, the other has no attainment to be measured by its standard.

Morality is an art and, as in every art, there is a form to be materialized and a matter to be formed. The finished work of art is the union of the two; artistic creation is the uniting of the two—the shaping of the matter and the embodying of the form. But, unless in Heaven, there is no finished moral product. In human history there is always new matter to be formed, and old morality to be reformed.

In morality, as in all art, the form must be fitted to the matter, as the matter to the form. The original material consists of human nature, human relations, and a physical environment; the form consists of organized harmony and co-operation. The task of the moral artist is to organize harmony and co-operation where they do not exist, and a more perfect harmony and co-operation where they already exist imperfectly. In executing this task the moralist, whether he be statesman, jurist, or economist, or the citizen performing the functions of all three, has to take account of the matter and the partial achievements in hand. He has to work on these and with these, and his achievement will always bear their imprint. He has to take one step at a time, as the painter has to add successive brush strokes, or the builder has to lay block upon block. Like all art, morality is persistently patient. "Art is long," and of all arts, morality is the longest.

A moral society is not an organism in which the parts exist for the whole, but an organization in which the whole exists for the parts. It is an organization by and for persons. It can be formulated, imagined, or contemplated by one person, but it can be achieved only through the participation and reciprocity of many persons. To achieve a moralized society these persons have first to be taken as they are, and then induced, persuaded, educated, beguiled, and, if needs be, threatened or forced, until they are ready to play their parts. To create justice it does not suffice that one person should dream of justice; it does not even suffice that a person should behave justly by himself. No single person *can* behave justly, any more than any single person can co-operate, discuss, or enjoy friendship.

The art of morality must embrace actions which in themselves are not morally ideal, but are designed to bring about that state of affairs in which the ideal moral behavior is possible. There is a making of morality which is no more a part of the moral product than the brush strokes are a part of the picture, or the laying of blocks a part of the building, or the action of the producer a part of the play.

But these analogies are misleading if pressed too far. The fact is that the moral being is both producer and actor. He has a double duty, to produce a moral order, and to behave in the manner which that order prescribes, and these two duties must somehow be made consistent; otherwise we shall find ourselves in the untenable position of saying that it is sometimes right to do wrong. We can avoid this bewilderment only by describing right action as that which conforms to ideal requirements so far as such conformity will at the same time help to realize these ideal requirements in life or in society at large.

We sometimes reluctantly concede that Communism and even Nazism are dynamic, whereas democracy is static. We mean that Communism and Nazism, being revolutionary, are embued with a sense of making and not merely a sense of being. We, the exponents of democracy, are too much inclined to pride ourselves on what we are. It would be fitter if we said not that we are a democracy, but that we are engaged in building a democracy, that democracy is our project—begun but not finished. Thanks to advancing science and technology, man has achieved "a unity of dwelling place"—the rooms connected by corridors, and equipped with fixtures. We are now hoping to dwell there in peace and plenty. The magnitude and the difficulty of this task should not dismay Americans. It agrees with a characteristic American habit of mind—namely, to associate morality with getting results, and to relish success, however difficult.[14] The creation of a moral order out of given materials, the taking account of existing conditions, the utilization of existing means and the invention of better, should be congenial to this habit of mind. It is more American to make a utopia than to dream of it or live in it. It would be American to improve and modernize Heaven rather than to enjoy it for a static eternity.

It is of the essence of the moral man that he is on his way, somewhere between what is and what ought to be. It is the essence of the moral art to advance like the walker, by friction and leverage of the ground beneath the feet, while imagining a destination beyond the range of sense. The art of morality is an ordered series of steps, in which each in turn is adapted to the last—from here to there and thence toward a remoter beyond. Such morality is neither despairing nor self-satisfied, but confident; neither merely theoretical nor merely practical, but intelligent.

The founding fathers founded, and their children have been building, a social order designed to yield abundant fruits of welfare and development for all its members, under their own control and direction. We are again engaged in founding and in building, this time of a wider society which shall stand in similar relations to its more numerous members. To this vast and exacting labor, to this immense and long-lasting enterprise, we are all called upon to bring our share of patience, firmness, and intelligent contrivance. There must be many builders, each with his own skill, and each with his own assignment. We must make a polity, law, and economy, a culture, education, and religion, suited to the spaciousness of the new structure. Its architecture is moral—a system of harmony and cooperation. This broad architectural design, suited to its general function, and to which all other institutions must conform, is entrusted to that institution which is called conscience. It is conscience which cherishes and keeps alive the underlying moral purpose of the whole. It consists of emotional attitudes, judgments, dispositions to performance, and habits of action, in which the inclusive good of all is set above the exclusive good of each.

If we ask ourselves why one state hesitates to break a treaty with another state, we find, in the first place, that it is moved by a fear of isolation. A state which breaks a treaty not only loses its reciprocal benefits, but acquires a reputation of untrustworthiness which disqualifies it for future treaties with the same or other nations. It thus forfeits the benefits of agreement and solidarity of action; which, since these are moral benefits, are moral motives, albeit on the comparatively low level of prudence.

This state is deterred by the opinion of neutral states, whose friendship it may someday need. This opinion of neutrals may reflect their own self-interest, or that disinterestedness which exists in some degree in all nations, and which is felt more strongly if they are not parties to the dispute. This "conscience of mankind" is not only moral, but is also a force. It carries not only a hint of hostility and menace which is feared by the offending party, but an appeal to higher motives which the offending party shares. The respect which is felt for the moral sentiment and opinion of the world is thus at the same time a respect of the offending party for itself. No nation can violate the moral approval of mankind without being divided at home as well as abroad.

Conscience, which speaks in each man's breast and therefore in all nations of men, is the only secure foundation for a world-wide concert of action. If this conscience is to be effective, it must be articulate and audible, deepseated and pervasive. Thus if the United States and the Soviet Union are to work together for the common good, the approvals and the disapprovals of their peoples must largely coincide. This holds of the United States and the British Commonwealth, and all around the circle. Where such a common conscience is lacking, it must be created, by distinguishing essentials from nonessentials and by finding a deeper common ground beneath superficial differences. This common ground, being discovered, must be perpetually reaffirmed and cultivated until the two peoples are governed by a strong sense of moral partnership, as the joint friends of justice and humanity.

Conscience is an expression of morality, but it needs to be perpetually refreshed and amended. It may serve its moral function imperfectly, and become, at some level of imperfection, crystallized and automatic. The inner moral motive may die, leaving only the outer shell. The critical, innovating moral faculty which sits in judgment even on conscience is called reason; or, in its specific moral application, the practical reason. This is the faculty with which the individual judges what end is good, and what means, serving that end, are right. In the household of morality this is the faculty which checks the accounts, introduces improvements, reorganizes, or expands—as when the international is added to the national. However its voice may be drowned in society at large, it speaks audibly at strategic points, in the minds of responsible statesmen and religious or moral leaders, and in the lucid intervals of all those who think for themselves.

The sanctions so far enumerated are moral in their motivation—in the inducements which they offer to choice, and by which they constrain men to obey the law. World-wide conscience is the basic achievement, only partial but already revealing its form, which underlies all other achievements—political, legal, cultural, educational, and religious—which in their sum will constitute that moral unity of man's world for which the unity of his dwelling place has paved the way.

CHAPTER THREE

Political Frame of World Order

HUMAN institutions are forms of organization by which human interests are brought into harmonious and fruitful relationships. And no institution can escape morality, for all institutions determine a man's conduct and its consequences for other men, and the ultimate norm of such interhuman dealings, whoever the man and whatever the dealings, is morality. They share to a greater or less degree this basic moral purpose. It is evident that morality itself cannot be derived from institutions, for if that were so, then it would be meaningless to say that any institution or any set of institutions ought to exist. There could be no good reason for institutions if the institutions themselves provided the reasons.

A state or polity is a society which, having many other bonds of unity, is also bound together by a common government. The art of government is politics, and its study is political science. The word "politics" is unhappily used to refer to the tricks of the trade and to the shady side of government rather than to its moral purpose; but in its classic meaning politics is so close to morality as to be, in the minds of some great philosophers, such as Plato and Aristotle, the same thing.

The so-called compact or contract theory of government means that government, however it may have originated, is not a biological or historical fatality in which men find themselves entrapped, but an instrument which is perpetuated by men because they find it useful and desirable. If they have not made it in the first instance, they can at least unmake it, unless they have good reasons for keeping it. They can ask themselves whether if they did not have a government, they would choose to create one; and if so, why.

Government is so closely associated with law that many legal writers are disposed to define polity in terms of law, while political writers often define law in terms of polity. But these identities obscure the distinct contribution which each institution makes to a well-organized society. If government and law were the same thing, then it could mean nothing to speak of a government of laws, as distinguished from a government of men. A good government will make laws, abide by laws, and execute laws. A personal and arbitrary government is not as good as a government of laws, but, for what it is worth, it is a government notwithstanding.

The practical reason for having a government of some kind is to be found in the need of a *central direction* of human affairs if they are to be conducted with the minimum of friction and the maximum of fruitfulness. If men are to be prevented from harming and destroying one another, there must be some decision between them other than force; and the decision must be accepted by the parties concerned. If men are to do *together* those things which they cannot do *alone,* again they need a central direction, and the direction must be followed. There must be a common policy which represents all particular interests and to which they are conformed. At the moment of action there must be a voice that speaks in behalf of all, is heard by all, and followed by all.

Since the vocabulary of government is commonly used to describe any form of control, so that we speak of the rule of reason or conscience and of the government of appetites by the will, polity in the strict sense requires a further qualification. The control must be vested in a separate human agency maintained for the purpose and having its own personnel. There must be not only government, but *a* government. The head is a person or persons having other organs besides a head; and the governed also have heads. In a prepolitical or nonpolitical condition of man, sometimes referred to as the state of nature, there is government in the broad sense of control, but the control is a part of every man's business and is not the whole of any man's business. The control is unified only through the fact that all men having the same reason and conscience are supposed to make the same decisions. A similar control is provided for insect societies through their identical or complementary instincts.

When, as in human government, the function of government is assumed by a special person or personnel, the relation between the ruler and the ruled is external. It is this which gives rise to the deep suspicion of the government by the governed, and their insistence upon having guarantees that it will not use its power for private rather than for public ends. It is this which leads the governed, having heads of their own, to retain the ultimate control in their own hands.

It will be noted that this definition of government leaves room for better governments and worse, and for many different arrangements by which the broad purpose of government is realized. It is said that a government is not a government unless it is obeyed—which is true. But obedience may be given to a freely elected official, or a hereditary monarch, or even to a tyrant. The ultimate decisions of government may be rendered by a representative parliament, by a court of judges, or by a hereditary king or ruling class. All government provides leadership and unity of action; but such leadership may prevail through fear or through persuasion. A government is no government at all unless it keeps the peace among the people over whom it rules, and enables them to act collectively; but the order which it establishes may be harsh and restrictive, or it may be liberal; it may be reactionary or progressive, partial or disinterested.

A definition of government should be such as to describe real governments and at the same time reveal the political ideal by which real governments can be compared and judged. To Lincoln the war against the South was something more than an assertion of the power of the existing government, something more, even, than the preservation of the Union. In his message to Congress on July 4, 1861, he said:

On the side of the Union it is a struggle for maintaining in the world that form and substance of government whose leading object is to elevate the condition of men—to lift artificial weights from all shoulders; to clear the paths of laudable pursuit for all; to afford all an unfettered start, and a fair chance in the race of life. Yielding to partial and temporary departures, from necessity, this is the leading object of the government for whose existence we contend.[1]

It is evident that Lincoln believed that the government over which he presided was not only a government having jurisdiction over the whole territory of the United States, and commanding its obedience, but at the same time a government whose "form" realized to a high degree that moral purpose which is the "substance" of government, so that those who were compelled to obey it had no sound reason for withholding their obedience. The South, he thought, had no legitimate complaint against the United States Government, since it gave them what a government is designed to give.

Morality may begin at home, but it does not end there. It is begotten by the relations between man and men, whoever they are and whatever their interests. Its obligations apply to the conduct of one man toward another regardless of existing differences of nation, race, or government—regardless of any difference whatsoever provided they both are men. Morally the murder of a Pole by a German is no less murderous than the murder of one German by another German; the theft of a foreigner's property is no less larcenous than the theft of the property of a fellow national; and the same is true of every item in the inventory of crimes and vices. Wherever human relations are extended, morality has jurisdiction, and it is then in order to construct the requisite institutions by which it may be carried into effect.

This truth is simple and incontrovertible. Why, then, does it need to be argued? How can it be that the notoriously immoral conduct between one politically organized society and another has been judged so leniently or even accepted by mankind with an untroubled conscience? The reasons, though they are not valid, are instructive.

In the first place, the conduct of an individual toward an alien is commonly governed by some collective purpose. If one individual living on one side of a political frontier murders or robs another individual living on the other side, his moral condemnation is clear. He is called a marauder, a pirate, or a bandit. When, however, the same homicidal or larcenous acts are performed by an agency of organized society, they are described by more ambiguous terms such as "war" or "Lebensraum." This is not because wholesale wickedness seems less wicked than small-scale wickedness, but because doubts arise as to the seat of responsibility. Furthermore, the individual who acts as a member of an organized society, however bloody and treacherous he may be toward the alien, is ordinarily loyal, co-operative, and even unselfish toward his own associates. He is forgiven his immorality in the larger sphere on account of his morality in the narrower. And the moral tribunal before which his case is tried is commonly made up of those who profit by his rectitude at home rather than of those who suffer from his transgressions abroad.

This explains, but it does not excuse. If it did, it would exonerate an honorable body of thieves who preyed upon society, or a good family man who maltreated his neighbors, or a loyal corporate official who cheated his rivals, or a regional partisan who defeated the good of the nation. The difficulties created by this series of concentric enclosures, with its narrower and its wider moralities, are the same all along the line and have to be conformed to the same principle—that morality does not end at any boundary short of the round earth. And if men or their like should be discovered on the planet Mars—beings with interests at stake and capable of coming to agreement with the inhabitants of Earth—then morality with its rights and wrongs would bridge the interstellar space. Happily that is a problem which we are not yet called upon to face.

A second reason for supposing that morality stops at political boundaries is the habit of regarding foreigners as implacable enemies. Even the domestic order provides for the private .use of violence in the last extremity of self-preservation. The past behavior of organized societies toward one another has not unnaturally begotten the idea that each is exposed to attack from the rest, and may therefore invoke the so-called right of self-preservation not only in occasional extremities, but as the basis of permanent policy.

This unhappy state of affairs, in which societies composed largely of decent and orderly individuals treat one another as beasts, and are perpetually haunted by mutual fears and suspicions, has been sufficiently experienced in recent decades to need no exposition here. The moral, however, is not its acceptance as a finality and the adoption of the maxim of cutting the other's throat lest he cut yours, but such organization of intersocietal relations as shall beget mutual confidence. The fact that organized societies are still living together in a state of sin, without benefit of morality, is not to be taken as a premise by which to justify disorderly conduct, but as presenting on a world-wide scale, and with evil consequences of corresponding magnitude, the very problem which morality is designed to solve.

Finally, however, there is a philosophy which in the name of morality itself expressly denies that the relations between politically organized societies are subject to moral jurisdiction. States, it is alleged, are not subject to morality, but above it. The state is like God in theological ethics —it makes things right by willing them. The individual's only moral obligation is obedience to the state; he has no duty to anyone outside that state of which he is a member, unless by its command. The state is the keeper of his conscience and the bearer of full responsibility for the consequences of his obedience.

This strange philosophy plays an important role in modern political theory. It is the last extravagance of nationalism. Suffice it here to say that, like other authoritarianisms, it is indefensible because it substitutes power for right and the arbitrary for the reasonable; and it is the worst of all authoritarianisms because it singles out for deification a being that is peculiarly unworthy of the role.

If morality by its very nature applies between man and man universally, if its rights and wrongs, its oughts and ought-nots, hold of any human act that directly or indirectly affects any human interest, then the same moral reason which argues for polity in a single society argues for a polity embracing all societies. The destructive conflicts between man and man and the opportunity of good through united effort, which form the basis of the limited polity, form the moral basis of an unlimited polity. The propinquity and the interdependence of *all* men now creates the same problem as that created by the propinquity and the interdependence of some men: like problem, like solution. The conditions, the goal, the instruments, are broadly the same.

This is an old idea, new only in the urgency of its application. Among its great exponents is Kant, who wrote as follows in that same eighteenth century which witnessed the birth of American democratic institutions:

Any one State must expect from any other the same sort of evils as oppressed individual men and compelled them to enter into a civil union regulated by law. Nature has accordingly again used the unsociableness of men, and even of great societies and political bodies . . . as a means to work out through their mutual antagonism a condition of rest and security. . . .

And, at last, after many devastations, overthrows and even complete internal exhaustion of their powers, the nations are driven forward to the goal which reason might easily have impressed upon them, even without so much sad experience. This is none other than the advance out of the lawless state of savages and the entering into a federation of nations. . . .

However visionary this idea may appear to be . . . it is nevertheless the inevitable issue of the necessity in which men involve one another. For this necessity must compel the nations to the very resolution—however hard it may appear—to which the savage in his uncivilized state was so unwillingly compelled when he had to surrender his brutal liberty and seek rest and security in a constitution regulated by law.[2]

Thus, according to Kant, man is driven by his "unsocial sociability" first to the civil order in which the liberty of each individual is limited "in order that it may coexist with the liberty of others"; and then to a "cosmopolitical" order in which the same principle is extended to the relations between nations.[3] There is no doubt of Kant's fundamental individualism. The "cosmopolitical" order is an order among civil polities each of which is an order of individual liberties.

This is a crucial point. The blessed term "international" has its grave dangers. It has acquired currency since the development of the modern nation-state, and reflects a nationalist way of thinking. It suggests that the nation-state is the ultimate term of the international polity, as the human individual is the ultimate term of the civil polity.

The truth is that the nation-state has no moral claims whatsoever except insofar as it represents the claims of its individual members. A recent writer has called attention to the following individual freedoms which it is the purpose of the United Nations to realize:

Freedom of speech and expression
Freedom of religion and worship
Freedom to travel on the high seas
Freedom to trade
Freedom to exercise an influence against transfer of the territory on which one lives
Freedom to influence the form of government to which one is subject
Freedom from fear, including freedom from war and invasion, from excessive armament burdens, and from tyrannical government
Freedom from want, involving improved labor standards, economic advancement, and social security [4]

It is clear that these freedoms are to be enjoyed not by the rulers, or by the nation-state in its corporate capacity, but by the peoples severally. The same is true of all benefits which a world polity is designed to secure. When they are shared by all, or a large number, of the members of a nation-state, they may for brevity of language be imputed to the nation-state as a whole. But when we justify world polity by the good it yields, and deem it right to create such a world polity, we must in the end appeal to the needs, the wants, the hopes, the aspirations, of the only beings that enjoy happiness or suffer unhappiness; namely, individual men and women.

The same individuals to whom international polity owes its benefits are also the sources of its legitimate power. It is to be noted that the compact or contract theory of government is the only theory that fits the case of international polity. Whatever may be true of the nation-state, international polity is not a biological or a historical necessity, which men inherit, but an arrangement which they voluntarily adopt for the sake of benefits to be received. We are now planning to enter into such an arrangement, and we hope eventually to profit by it—we, and our children, and children's children.

It is unfortunate that the name "international" should be used for the all-embracing human polity, but fortunate that when it is now used, it is with the emphasis on the "inter" rather than the "national." The moral proof of world polity rests on two principles: personality and universality, the claim of the individual man, and the equal claims of all men. Morally speaking, the nation-state is a historical accident. The essential purpose and meaning of polity—harmony and co-operation achieved by common policy—does not prescribe that men shall live under that limited form of polity which stands somewhere midway between the individual person and the polity of all persons. It is quite conceivable that human history should have begun with a single all-embracing polity, and that as this grew in magnitude and complexity it should have been decentralized and divided into subpolities, each united within by its local peculiarities. History has sometimes moved in this direction, as in the dismemberment of empires. History has sometimes moved in the opposite direction, as in the creation of the modern European states out of lesser ethnic or feudal units. It is in this direction that we now propose to move further, from the nation-state to a global polity which is called international because it starts with national polities and seeks to introduce unity among them.

To say that the national polity is a historical accident reveals the bare bones of the argument. It does not in the least belittle the practical importance of the nation-state.

It may well be that the nation-state represents the most important single step in the political evolution of man and deserves to be honored accordingly. It may be that a world polity would be impossible had not the chief part of political organization been already achieved within the national polity. Or, on the other hand, it may prove that the role of the nation-state has been exaggerated, and that something of what it has done must needs be undone.

Whether the world polity should take the form of a highly centralized control, describable as a superstate or a federal union; or of an intimate interweaving of interests describable as a world community; or of concurrent action by national governments—this is not a question of principle, but of method and degree. The principle is that there shall be a world policy adopted, proclaimed, and obeyed; and that this policy shall embrace so much of human affairs as may be necessary to prevent conflict, and to provide facilities of co-operation wherever world-wide co-operation is more fruitful of good than single-handedness, or than co-operation within a more limited sphere.

A polity of international dimensions is to be judged by the same standards as a lesser polity, having the same purpose and being liable to the same failures and abuses. It is designed to impose on its members a united policy which shall express and serve their several interests. A government may fail to serve men's interests adequately through neglect or inefficiency. It may fail to express men's interests through becoming arbitrary or paternalistic. It may abuse its authority through subordinating the public interest to the private interest of the ruler. An international government can be bad in every way in which any government can be bad; and it is not less bad for being international.

An international polity has its own peculiar political

{ *78* }

dangers, owing to its remoteness from the individuals who are the rightful sources of its authority and the rightful claimants of its benefits. There are peculiar dangers which arise from the fact that an international government deals with governments. It is disposed to accept without question the authority of the national government over its own peoples, and to be more concerned that it should be firm and stable than that it should be freely chosen. International government may by strengthening a national government strengthen its power *against* its own people, as when reactionary monarchs conspire to suppress revolution. Or an international government which dispenses its benefits through national governments may not concern itself at all with the distribution of these benefits to the peoples of the nations. It may actually benefit only the national rulers or other selfish interests with which the rulers are most closely associated.

The only international government which is morally justified is that in which the national government serves as a channel by which power ascends from the people, and by which benefits descend to the people.

Recent discussions of world polity have focused attention upon the use of force, and have obscured the fact that while the use of force may sometimes, as at present, be an imperative necessity, it is evidence of the failure of polity rather than of its success. Conceived in terms of its moral purpose, polity is a form of organization in which the resort to force is no longer necessary. This has been recognized by all political thinkers, save only those who regard the exercise of force as an end in itself. In Christian thought the use of penalties by a divine ruler is explained by man's fall. If man had continued, as he ought, to love

God, there would have been no need of coercion; but the Kingdom of God would have been all the more perfect. Similarly, if the reason and conscience of man had been sufficiently strong, the kingdom of man would have been perfected without resort to intimidation.

It is right and reasonable for all parties to come to agreement—in order to escape the evils of conflict and reap the benefits of co-operation. Unhappily, however, there are men who fail to see this, or who, seeing it, fail to act accordingly. Such men have to be offered other and lower inducements, in the form of penalties, to bring them into line. Otherwise they will deprive those who agree of the benefits of their agreement; and will take advantage of those who, having agreed among themselves, have renounced the use of force and have thrown away their arms.

When this principle is applied internally, within any given civil order, the private use of force retires into the background, as a last resort which is rarely invoked. The government, drawing upon the collective force and having an unlimited drawing account, intervenes against those who refuse to agree, or who break their agreement, actual or tacit; it protects those who do agree in the enjoyment of the benefits of their agreement. But the collective force is so overwhelming that it is rarely used. It is sufficient that it should be made available and that the intent to use it should be known. To those who would disobey the government if they dared, it acts as a deterrent; to those who share the purpose of the government and obey it willingly, it provides the necessary "security" against the disobedience of others.

The use of force by a world polity is based on the analogy of civil polity. The nations enter into agreement in order to avoid armed conflict and in order to share the benefits of co-operation. No nation can afford to give up its resort to force unless it has a guarantee that other nations will do likewise. It cannot rely wholly on the goodwill and good faith of other nations, and is obliged to create a collective force which will check or penalize those who will not enter or keep the agreement. In other words, the "peace-loving" nations who renounce the use of force have to be protected against "aggressor" nations who have not yet been converted to the love of peace, or who, having been converted, may at some future time lapse into aggression. The international force, drawing upon the forces of all nations, should then be so overwhelming that the mere threat of its use would ordinarily be sufficient to deter a would-be aggressor. The hopelessness of aggression would in time beget a habit of peacefulness; and the international polity, like the civil polity, would then be obeyed from a mixture of motives—prudence, habit, and reason. In a perfected international order nations would agree because they saw that it was right and reasonable to agree; or because they shared and respected the conscience and reason of mankind at large.

The use of force is secondary in practice as well as in theory. There must be an agreement not to use force except collectively for the common purposes of peace and co-operation; and there must be an agreement to employ the methods of law, negotiation, and arbitration for settling disputes. Neither of these agreements can be forced. Force is now being used against the enemy, conceived as the aggressor. Force must be used against this or any similar enemy so long as he refuses to come to agreement. But force, while it may render him harmless, cannot make him agree, or convert his selfish will into goodwill. Only persuasion, if anything, can do that. Meanwhile the professed friends of a peaceful and fruitful world order are by thought, books, speeches, discussions, conferences, endeavoring to persuade themselves and one another, so as to create a firm and unified will. Only insofar as that will is created and perpetuated can its object—a peaceful and fruitful world order—be actualized.

The international polity cannot be justified on the ground of national selfishness, however enlightened. A recent letter to the press written by an official of the State Department and member of the Council of the Foreign Policy Association informs the public that " 'disinterested benevolence' . . . while it is a noble human attribute . . . obviously has no place whatever in the foreign policy of any National Government"; and supports this shocking statement by comparing national government with the directors of a business corporation whose objective is "to earn maximum profits for the shareholders for whom they are trustees, by engaging in such legal and proper corporate activities as in their judgment are conducive to that end." [5] But by the writer's own admission the corporate director is controlled by what is "legal and proper." This lets the moral cat out of the bag! "Legal and proper" means what is good for the country as a whole, as distinguished from private selfishness. Insofar as the directors accept this control willingly, and share its public purpose, they are disinterestedly benevolent, however much they may shrink from being considered "noble." The government of a nation has the same obligation to subordinate the national selfishness to what is internationally "legal and proper."

It is war and not peace which is designed to serve one national interest, regardless of the cost to other nations.

The world order cannot give, and should not promise to give, to each nation that which it covets. In giving to all it must limit what it gives to each. To take the simplest possible example, suppose a nation to desire territorial expansion—a nation whose nationalism is of the sort described as "not so much love of country as love of *more* country." [6] Such nations have been known to exist. It is self-evident that as the surface of the earth is now divided, territory which is acquired has to be taken away from somebody. A territorially greedy nation would therefore *not* gain its territorial ends by a world order which respected the claims of all existing proprietors and did justice between them.

It is quite true that some national interests are served by a just international order. Portions, at least, of a national economy are benefited by a rise in the standard of living abroad. A just world order gives freedom from fear to every nation, and its peacetime interests will profit accordingly. The appeal to national self-interest can be supported by this evidence, as far as it goes. But there is also evidence to the contrary. A nation that prefers conquest to trade, or that sets military glory above all the other values of life, will *not* benefit by a world order; and will, if actuated by enlightened selfishness, seek to prevent its creation.

Whether the self-interest of a nation would or would not be promoted by a just world order depends on the kind of nation it is, or on what it conceives its interests to be. The real problem is to persuade a nation to identify itself with the kind of interest which profits by harmony rather than by conflict, and by co-operation rather than by isolation.

Nothing could be vaguer or more meaningless than "national interest" as conceived by those who most glibly prate about it. Is it the interest of the government, or the interest of the governed? Is it the interest of all the governed, or only some of the governed? Or is it the interest of the nation as a whole as distinguished from the interests of its members taken severally? These may be very different. A nation as a whole may occupy a continent without any member's occupying so much as an acre; it may possess vast natural resources when most of its members live in poverty; it may have the power to impose its will on other nations when its individual members are enslaved.

We hear much in these days of "power" as a national interest. Indeed it is customary to speak of politically organized societies as "powers" rather than as states or even as nations. So named, polities are classified as "small powers," "great powers," and "superpowers." The idea needs deflating. It measures polities in terms of their capacity to wage war and to exert influence through fear. It is true that such capacity reflects industrial development as well as manpower and military skill. It is true that it requires unity and discipline. But greatness of power abroad is quite consistent with economic exploitation or political tyranny at home; unity may be obtained by false propaganda, and discipline by intimidation. It is possible for a nation to be great in war without being great in peace or great in the hearts of its countrymen. So while greatness of military power is a fact which must be soberly recognized as a condition of action, it should not be confused with greatness as a standard of excellence. The terms "power" and "great" used without further qualification carry emotional overtones of eulogy. They should never be used without specification. Great in *what?* Power *for* what? Greatness of size is one thing, or as many things as are quantitatively measurable; greatness of quality is an-

other thing. Greatness of soul is very different from greatness of body. Power for war is different from power for
peace. Greatness is good only when it is great in goodness;
power is good only when it is powerful for good. In themselves greatness and power imply no values whatsoever.

The late Professor Spykman has said, in effect, that a
nation in its relations with other nations should be governed only by the motive of power:

> The statesman who conducts foreign policy can concern
> himself with values of justice, fairness, and tolerance only to
> the extent that they contribute to or do not interfere with the
> power objective. They can be used instrumentally as moral
> justification for the power quest, but they must be discarded
> the moment their application brings weakness. The search for
> power is not made for the achievement of moral values; moral
> values are used to facilitate the attainment of power.[7]

What does this writer mean by the "power objective"?
Evidently, military power. He puts military power above
"justice, fairness, and tolerance." By what standard, then,
does he evaluate military power? Apparently by no standard, thus defying the fact that moral standards apply in-
escapably and by their very meaning to all human conduct.
A nation which does not behave justly, fairly, and tol-
erantly is unjust, unfair, and intolerant, with the condemnation which these terms imply. What does this writer
mean by "can" and "must"? Does he mean to describe the
way in which a nation's foreign affairs *are* conducted? In
that case there is a moral obligation to find a better way.
Does he mean to state the way in which they *ought* to be
conducted? In that case he is both dogmatic and gravely
mistaken. In all probability Professor Spykman means
both, and would have us believe that in political matters

what ought to be is what is; in which case he is, again, gravely mistaken.

There are nations which are great in war, and in which that form of greatness is esteemed above all other forms. There are intermediate powers, such as France, Poland, and Italy, which would like to be great in war, and which suffer from a sense of frustration because they have lost or not yet achieved that form of greatness. Perhaps it would be more just to say that all nations are in some degree tainted with this false pride, longing for a military power which they do not have or fearful of losing what they have. Insofar as nations are motivated by such ambitions they may be termed warlike or militaristic; their pride is false because it has nothing to do with their goodness, or with the things of which they have reason to be proud.

There are, on the other hand, nations which are weak in war and have no cause for shame. Athens after it had ceased to be an empire and Germany before it became an empire are cases in point. Also, Switzerland and the Scandinavian powers. Such nations can be *justly* proud; their self-esteem is based on their contributions to human happiness and civilization. Finally, there are those nations which, while being great in war, esteem this kind of greatness only as an instrument of good or as a regrettable necessity in time of trouble. Such nations may be war-making while still peace-loving nations. And it may be granted that there is a strain of this peace-loving in all nations.

Insofar as a nation is warlike or militaristic, its self-interest would be defeated, and not served, by a just and peaceful world. Its violence would then be obsolete; its military virtues would be at a discount; its pride would be mere bombast; its hopes of conquest and subjugation would be forever defeated; its kind of greatness would receive no recognition or applause. It would wear the aspect of a caged carnivore or of an ex-prize fighter. The enlightened pursuit of self-interest would impel such a nation to employ every available means to prevent the creation of a world in which *its* kind of national self could have no place.

Insofar, on the other hand, as a nation is practiced in the arts of peace, and devoted to that just well-being of its people which only peace permits, it will promote peace and welcome its advent. Insofar as people are humane and enjoy friendship, preferring common goods to exclusive gains, a nation will promote and welcome co-operation on a world-wide scale. The powerful peace-loving nation will be willing that its military chieftains, idolized in the hour of extremity, be reduced to less heroic proportions; and that its power be measured in terms of responsibility rather than glory. Such a nation will forgo the use of force to gain its ends, because neither the exercise nor the results of force are relished. It has been said that Hitler acquired by force what the Weimar Republic failed to acquire by conciliation. It is impossible to acquire by force what is acquired by conciliation—since the first acquires hardness of heart, fear, and resentment, while the other acquires understanding and agreement.

In short, if nations are to be persuaded to support a moral unity of the world, appeal to their self-interest must beget a newer and higher self-interest, and not merely implement the old. The purpose of the appeal should be to generate the kind of self-interest the enlightened realization of which will be generally beneficent, or which will fit a world based on justice and humanity. Insofar as nations are peace-loving, enlightenment will suffice. Insofar as they are warlike and militaristic, they must first be made peace-loving. Nazism, for example, is not a lack of enlightenment, but a set of values falsely esteemed; whereas democracy, because, and only because, its ends are good, can find its salvation through a more enlightened choice of means.

National interest is commonly believed to embrace political autonomy, or the so-called right of self-determination. This issue is forced by the general political instability, the fluidity of boundaries, the revival of old grievances felt by oppressed minorities and frustrated nationalisms, the rise of new nationalisms within old empires, and the occupation of liberated and enemy territory by the victors. Apart from these immediate problems of "settlement," there is the general question whether the proposed international polity should be used to multiply and protect national polities, or to reduce their number, taking account of their growing interdependence.

Loose thinking confuses the claim of a people to their own government with the claim of a government to have or own its people—which is something very different. It so happens that certain governments have recently resided in London or Cairo, separated from their peoples residing on the continent of Europe. Now that the time has come for bringing together governments and peoples, it has proved necessary to decide where the right of possession resides. There is little doubt of the answer. There is no just claim of an unemployed government to a job of governing. But, as a recent writer has said, "a sound internationalism and good humanism will be concerned for little people, human beings, and not peculiarly for little states." [8]

There is no right of a government either to the people

of another government, or to its own people. The right runs the other way. The people have a right to their own government—that is, to a government of their own choosing. Just when a government can be said to be chosen by its own people is not easy to determine—whether by free elections or by some more informal expression of popular opinion and sentiment. But it is clear that a people cannot be said to have its own government merely because it was chosen at some time in the past, or because it speaks in their name, or because it has some technical claim to "legitimacy." A government is its people's government so long as they continue to choose it, when its mandate is perpetually renewed, so that it can be said to be an instrument of self-government by which persons realize their ruling faculties and are the custodians and guardians of their own interests.

This conclusion, however, leaves open a further and more troublesome question. The principle of self-determination is commonly claimed by a minority which already has a government which it shares with others, but which it desires to replace by a separate government of its own. If the existing government can be said to give effective expression to the choice of the whole people, without discrimination, then the minority has no case; to concede its right of secession would mean the end of all popular government, which requires that a defeated minority shall submit, provided they have had an equal opportunity with all other groups to influence the outcome. It is their government even when, as the voice of all, it rules against them. This is precisely the ground taken by Lincoln when he held that the South, having participated in the choice of the existing government, could not invoke the principle of self-government in defense of their disobedience. They were pursuing a course which would lead to a progressive disintegration, reverse the whole process of political organization, and undo its benefits:

> Self-determination, which has nothing to do with self-government but has become confused with it, is barbarous and reactionary: by sanctioning secession, it invites majorities and minorities to be intransigent and irreconcilable. It is stipulated in the principle of self-determination that they need not be compatriots because they will soon be aliens. There is no end to this atomization of human society. Within the minorities who have seceded there will tend to appear other minorities who in their turn will wish to secede.[9]

When, on the other hand, a minority has good ground for claiming that the existing government, because of its distance, or its racial or cultural differences, or its tyrannical abuses, is not their own and fails to give them self-government, then its grievance can be met in either of two ways: either by reforming the government or by creating another government.

Which of these remedies should be invoked? Assuming that they are popular governments, with free institutions enjoyed by all who live under them, should there be more national governments or fewer? It has been said that the peace treaties which followed the First World War encouraged the rise of new nation-states without providing any international system within which they could exist and prosper. But there still remains the fundamental question whether the trend should be toward consolidation or toward subdivision. Or should federalism, with its division between the functions of central and subordinate governments, be employed as a method of compromise? There is no categorical answer to this question. In view of local and historical conditions it is never twice the same question. There are, however, certain maxims which should be observed, and which, when observed, will often diminish the importance of the question even though they do not answer it.

First, rid men's minds of the superstitious and fictitious interests associated with a fanatical nationalism; or make men more mindful of their real interests.

Second, banish the wholly indefensible idea that any group is entitled to a separate government if they are willing to fight for it.

Third, be mindful of the fact that the multiplication of nation-states tends to increase rivalry and diminish agreement and co-operation.

Fourth, be mindful, on the other hand, that a common government can serve its purpose only when there is also a community of culture; and when the government is close to its people in understanding as well as in space.

Finally, recognize degrees of self-determination, permitting of semi-autonomy as well as complete autonomy, and making it possible to combine local self-government for some purposes with centralized government for other purposes.

When men desire to have a government of their own in place of a government which they share with others, they speak of self-determination. When having a government of their own they fear a supergovernment imposed upon them from above, they invoke the principle of sovereignty. The question of sovereignty has two applications, internal and external.[10] Where, as in popular government, the government exercises an authority delegated to it by the governed, the internal sovereignty is said to reside in the people. The government whose control is controlled does not possess sovereignty. It occupies the driver's seat, but obeys the instructions of the back-seat drivers. The people are sovereign *within* the polity. When, on the other hand, we speak of "sovereign nations," imputing sovereignty to a nation as a whole, government and governed alike, we refer to its external sovereignty. It is this last conception—tainted by error and infused with sentiment—that constitutes the chief obstacle to international political organization. It may mean only that its political controls from abroad are transmitted to its people through their own government. Or it may mean the *absence* of controls from abroad.

The question of external national sovereignty is divisible into two questions, the question of fact and the question of right. In both cases the merits of the argument are the reverse of what is commonly supposed.

In fact, no nation is or can be free from external controls. Being surrounded by other nations, it must make concessions to them, as it must make concessions to its natural environment. Since some degree of external control is inescapable, how shall it be reduced to a minimum for all nations? International organization is the answer to that question. As the autonomy of the individual is increased and not diminished by the civil order, so the autonomy of the nation-state is increased and not diminished by the international order. The principle is the same—that orderly freedom is greater than disorderly freedom, all individuals and all nations being considered.

The question of the nation's right to sovereignty is sometimes argued in terms of its alleged "personality." But this argument rests on a misleading analogy. The individual human being is a natural or real person—an indisputable fact which begins to be when the umbilical cord is severed. The individual person possesses certain inherent claims by virtue of his capacities for happiness, self-direction, and moral judgment. These claims are the primal source of all human rights. The nation-state, on the other hand, has at most a fictitious or imputed personality. Like the business corporation, it is a personality only insofar as it is so treated, or so regarded in the eyes of the law. Whether or not it should be so treated is an open question, which has to be decided in terms of the claims of its members—the natural or real persons of which it is composed. Whatever rights it possesses are derivative and secondary.

But whether primary or secondary, the right of national sovereignty is limited. There is no such thing as an unlimited right on any level, personal or national. The rightness of a right lies in its being embraced within a system of rights, in which the freedom of each is limited by the freedoms of all. Hence international organization *gives* a nation its rightful sovereignty, and does not take it away.

The expression "national sovereignty," as commonly used, does not signify a clearly ascertained fact, or a clearly defined right, but the more or less justifiable resistance of men to control from beyond themselves. It expresses in absolute and extreme terms what can and ought to be achieved only partially. Every agreement or treaty between one society and another, however narrow its scope or precarious its stability, is a control of each by the other. The fact that a treaty is made voluntarily means that each party deems it desirable to submit to control by the other; and the reserved right to renounce a treaty means only that a nation may change its mind, and substitute some other form of control without being guilty of breaking a promise. If there is to be a world polity, it must actually control what it purports to control; and what it controls is thereby taken away from the autonomous control of its parts. World polity is irreconcilable in fact or in right with the absolute sovereignty of the nation-state, if by absolute sovereignty is meant unlimited control; but the world polity may control so little that the control left to the nation-state is sufficient to satisfy that sentiment of independence of which the word "sovereignty" has become the symbol. It does not imply the fateful crossing of any sharp dividing line from inviolable national sovereignty to its violation.

The principles of self-determination and sovereignty sometimes appear in the form of an assurance to liberated countries that there will be no interference with their "internal affairs." Here again policy is translated into a flat formula which is contradicted both by the facts and even by the declared intent of the liberators. Events have proved what could have been anticipated, that it is not possible to occupy a territory, and assume control, without taking sides. Order cannot be restored without naming and opposing the internal faction that is taken to be the enemy of order, and this discrimination will inevitably reflect the political bias of those who assume control. Soviet Russia has never suffered any illusions on this subject. Great Britain and the United States have adopted a more faltering course, fitted neither to their professions nor to the facts, and therefore criticized both for its inconsistency in principle and its ineffectiveness in practice.

When the Allies liberated Italy, they declared that "nothing can detract from the absolute and untrammeled right of the people of Italy by *constitutional* means to decide on the *democratic* form of government they will eventually have." [11] When one first read this declaration one rubbed one's eyes—it was so flagrantly self-contradictory that it suggested a clerical error or bedevilment by the printer. But no—on May 24, 1944, in an address to the House of Commons, Prime Minister Churchill solemnly repeated the same riddle:

It is understood throughout Italy, and it is the firm intention of the United States, that Italy, like all other countries which are now associated with us, shall have fair and free opportunity, as soon as the Germans are driven out and tranquillity is restored, of deciding whatever form of democratic government, whether monarchical or republican, they desire.[12]

This declaration still further narrowed the untrammeled option. It promised to the people of Italy, provided they remained "tranquil," a free choice between the British system and the American system, with Soviet Russia keeping its hands off because it was not in this case doing the liberating. Similar pronouncements were afterward made by the American authorities, applied to other liberated regions, and so often repeated that their absurdity was concealed by their familiarity.

We had, in other words, the firm intention of doing the meaningless and the impossible. We proposed at one and the same time to abstain from interference and to intervene in behalf of tranquillity—to let the liberated peoples freely alone, and at the same time to compel them, by the influences at our command, to adopt a peculiar set of political institutions.

The confusion over interference and noninterference in a nation's internal affairs reflects a more fundamental confusion regarding the relation of domestic and foreign policy in general. Their separation is another of those false abstractions which having been made have to be aban-

doned, and meanwhile can result only in muddle and vac-
illation. Foreign affairs are domestic affairs at both ends.
It is impossible for a first nation to deal with a second nation at all—whether by conquest, temporary occupation,
diplomacy, treaty, or union in a common international
polity—without influencing the internal affairs of that nation. And the kind of influence which the first exerts upon
the second will reflect the way in which the first conducts
itself at home.

This remains a fact even if the primary object of international dealings is to alter international dealings. It is
still the nations which do the dealing and are dealt with;
and their international dealings, both in act and in effect,
will be a part of their national dealing. To suppose that
international affairs can be separated from intranational
affairs is as absurd as to suppose that the intercourse of two
persons can be separated from their two personalities, or
that the way a man lives in his own house can be divorced
from his treatment of and by his neighbors.

Whatever international political organization is created
will express the political ideas of those who create it, and
will regulate the political institutions of its members.
Wherever the Allies are in a position of responsibility,
they are bound to act in accordance with their political
beliefs, and to seek to induce like beliefs in those with
whom in the future they hope to live and work. They have
their own idea of what they call a "family of nations"; and
it is their purpose in this case to choose their relatives
according to specifications. This purpose may be construed
broadly or narrowly, and it may be carried into effect
abruptly or gradually, but there can be and should be no
doubt of the purpose.

This is the clue to the role of democracy in international

polity. The Atlantic Charter, the Four Freedoms, and all similar declarations of the United Nations are in substance democratic. They are rooted in the democratic traditions of the nations which formulated them. They apply abroad —in a more expanded form—the political standards which are professed, and in some measure applied, at home.

The proposed international polity is democratic in its inspiration. If it is created, it will be broadly democratic in its procedures, and if it is successful, it will be democratic in its effects. Those who join it and live up to its obligations must maintain, develop, and perfect their own domestic democratic institutions. Their governments must express the popular will, freely formed by discussion and the circulation of ideas. They must enjoy civil liberties at home if they are to be responsive to the public opinion of mankind and take part in its formation. They cannot associate themselves with all the races of the earth, and acknowledge their equal rights, and remain indifferent to race prejudice and discrimination within their own borders. They cannot participate in the lifting of burdens and the removal of disabilities throughout the world and take no measures for the relief of poverty, exploitation, illiteracy, malnutrition, and disease among their own people. Nations may be guilty of these inconsistencies and insincerities, but they will suffer from them, both in their international usefulness and in their national integrity.

In proportion as an international organization is morally justified, it will be a democratic organization of democracies. Democracy is the only form of polity which implies international organization as a phase of its own development. It is *in principle* applicable to all men. It is the only form of polity which is fit to be erected on the international scale, because it gives to nations, and does not take away; or takes away only in order to give more abundantly, and takes from one only in order to give to all, that one included. It is, therefore, the only kind of internationality which is consistent with the national aspirations of all nations. But it is ultimately mindful of persons, and of nations only so far as they serve the persons of whom they are composed. It is the essential purpose of democracy to encourage and protect each man and each group of men in the effective possession and enjoyment of freedom. It is designed to promote the maximum of diversity and autonomy which is consistent with order. Therefore its greater unities, up to and including a global unity, need not be feared. Its whole is the expression and the servant of its parts.

International polity is an enterprise, begun but not completed. The greater part of it is yet to be. It exists in men's minds, as a good to be attained in some future time. If it is not to remain there forever in the future, as something hoped for and imagined but perpetually postponed, hope and imagination must be accompanied by action. This present action must be idealistic in that it is directed to the good, and realistic in that it takes account of present conditions and makes use of present instruments. It would be fatal to allow a quarrel to break out between the architects and the builders; or to allow them to become so separated that the architects merely drew and exhibited plans while the builders busied themselves with merely moving and accumulating the blocks.

A sound, workable, and enduring international polity will take a long time to build. It is the most ambitious enterprise that men have ever undertaken. It will take every form of human talent, it will take the manpower of all mankind, and it will take time. It takes time to form habits, to reorganize men into new institutions, and to persuade men to adopt new ideas. The analogy of the blocks and the builders is misleading. The international polity is built of men; and, unlike blocks, men have to be induced to take their places and cannot be put in place by a derrick and kept in place by cement. They need to share the plans with the architect and the builders.

Men may properly be reproached for doing "too little too late." But they also need to be warned against expecting too much too soon. If they expect an international polity tomorrow, then when tomorrow comes they will lose heart and give up. Or, their minds leaping lightly to the end result, they will neglect the intermediate things which it is necessary to do. They will attempt to put on the roof before they have laid the foundations or erected the walls. They will fail to take that next step for which previous steps have paved the way, and which will pave the way to future steps. But it is also true that men cannot be induced to take any step unless they experience a sense of forward movement and can see the finished structure progressively emerge.

Toward that international polity which we seek to build we have certain present assets. There is a poignant sense of its need, begotten by the horrors of war and the fear of their repetition. We have national political institutions and national political experience. We have a legacy of ideas inherited from the political thinkers of the past. We have the lessons recently taught by an unsuccessful international polity—the League of Nations. We have an assured military victory over the present enemies of international polity. We have a unity of nations, forged in the heat of war and pledged to the work of peace. In the realm of action this is our greatest asset. The powerful nations which, having won the war, will exert the greatest influence and carry the heaviest burden of responsibility in the years to come are favorably disposed. Their self-interest, as they conceive it, is happily of the kind that needs no radical alteration in order to agree with the interest of all nations.

These assets must not be thrown away. They are what we have to work with, and all we have to work with. They must be used and at the same time conserved for use in the future. The unity already achieved between Soviet Russia, the British Commonwealth of Nations, France, China, and the United States—their capacity to work together and discuss their policies together, their agreement to agree as much as possible, and to resolve their disagreement—is a most precious achievement, and the best hope of future achievement. Peoples, as well as governments, should place this first, and speak no reckless word nor commit any reckless act that will place it in jeopardy.

At the same time that men and nations are engaged in building an international polity they must continue to live in such polities as they have—in national polities, with half-made or temporary linkages between. Each national government must protect the interests of its people by what methods are presently available, even when these are called bad names when compared with the methods of the better time to come. Nations cannot suspend their lives or their governments or their responsibility to their peoples until they can all be housed in the new international structure.

Those nations which now have the power to defend themselves, and which have proved that power in the bloody ordeal of war, cannot be expected to throw that power away. They cannot be expected to entrust their interests and safety to authorities which do not yet exist and may not for years to come be equal to the task.[13] It should be taken as a matter of course that diplomacy, alliances, spheres of influence, power politics, and national armaments will continue to be employed until the better alternative has come into being and proved itself in action. This is a general fact which should be candidly acknowledged by each nation for itself, and not charged reproachfully and self-righteously against other nations.

But such prudent continuation of old practices, obsolescent in thought but still necessary in action, should be progressively adapted to the new and better practice of the future. Its realism should be tempered, as well as directed, by idealism. To work *with* what one has, and at the same time work *for* what one hopes to have—this is the guiding principle of political progress. And mindful of the greatness of the task, we must applaud every forward gain. If we reserve our applause for the last and culminating victory, we shall never reach that ultimate victory, for lack of the zest and buoyancy to wage a long campaign. A small step toward a great goal borrows the greatness of its goal.

CHAPTER FOUR

The World-Wide Rule of Law

LAW is not the same as government, though the two tend to be identified because political scientists write about law and jurists write about government. If they were not different, it would be meaningless to speak of law without government, or government without law, or of that state of affairs, doubly blessed, in which the two are combined—a constitutional government founded on law and whose several branches make, execute, and interpret law.

Although the term "law" has many meanings which it is important to distinguish, there is also a fundamental meaning which these different meanings have in common and which justifies the common name. Law in this fundamental sense goes to the very roots of being and knowledge. It so happens that being is divisible into general and particular, and that it is therefore possible to know the particular by the general. The meaning of the distinction between general and particular troubles only the philosopher, and his readers may happily be spared its pains. For our present purposes it is sufficient to observe that whatever be the ultimate analysis of the matter, there is a difference between the moon in particular and body in general, between Socrates and man, between the triangle occasionally tapped by a certain member of the Boston

Symphony Orchestra and the geometrical triangle in which Euclid was interested.

We have next to note that several particulars—as many as may happen to exist—are subsumable under the same general: the earth also is a body; Pericles also is a man; there is also an instrument played in the New York Philharmonic which is a triangle.

And every particular is subsumable under two or more generals. The moon is a sphere as well as a body; Socrates is a citizen of Athens as well as a man; the musical instrument in question is a metal as well as a triangle. Or if we prefer to speak in terms of knowledge, the moon may be not only *perceived* in its particularity, but *conceived* in several different ways—as body and as sphere; similarly, Socrates may be conceived as man and as citizen, or the orchestral item as triangle or as metal. The moon's bodily character does not preclude its spherical character; Socrates' humanity does not preclude his citizenship; and the instrument's geometry does not stand in the way of its metallurgy. The generals have, in other words, logical or mathematical relations one to another—relations of consistency and implication. Owing to these so-called necessary relations, a particular subsumed under one general may or may not, must or must not, be subsumed also under certain other generals.

We have next to note, finally, that the general prescribes the behavior of its particulars. As goes the general, so go the particulars. When one knows the general or combination of generals under which a particular is subsumable, one can predict its behavior. The general is then said to constitute the law; and the particular's agreement with its general is termed its obedience.

We are now ready for the distinction which most concerns us here, the distinction, namely, between the kind of law the physicists teach, such as the law of gravitation, and the kind of law that is taught in law schools and practiced by lawyers, such as the law against homicide. The former is commonly called a "scientific law," because the expression "natural law" or "law of nature" has been pre-empted for another use. This is unfortunate, because it suggests that this kind of law resides in science rather than in the world which the scientist explores. The fundamental fact is that the events of nature conform to laws, and not that people called scientists invent laws. This holds of all law, that it is where it is obeyed. When it is merely thought about, imagined, hoped for, or otherwise entertained by the mind, it is a hypothesis. But waiving this possible misunderstanding, let us refer to the physicist's, chemist's, or mathematician's kind of law as "scientific law," and let us refer to the lawyer's kind of law as "jural law." What, then, is the difference?

In the first place, the jural law is obeyed voluntarily, while the scientific law may be, and usually is, obeyed involuntarily. Thus the bomber obeys military law voluntarily, the bomb obeys the law of chemistry involuntarily. That which obeys a jural law, namely, a person, obeys it by choice, and can choose to disobey it. Insofar as jural law is obeyed by habit, it resembles scientific law; if the sun chose to move or stand still, scientific law would resemble jural law.

In the second place, the intent of the scientific law is descriptive; the intent of the jural law is mandatory. Statements of scientific law use the words "is" or "does"; jural law employs the word "shall." The physicist is interested in finding the law which any given beings do obey; the jurist is interested in making beings that shall obey a given law. If a law is disobeyed, the scientist says "so much the worse for the law," or calls it a miracle; the jurist says "so much the worse for the man," and calls it a crime. If a law is disobeyed, the physicist looks for another law; the jurist looks for another being. If the moon disobeyed the law of gravity, the physicist would abandon the law in favor of a law of levity. If a man disobeyed the law against homicide, the jurist would try to make men nonhomicidal.

In the examples which have been used the scientific law is stated in positive terms, the jural law in negative terms. There is no difference of principle or logic. Nature could be described in terms of what events do *not* do; and men could be remade in terms of what they *shall* do. But it so happens that organized society has heretofore been especially interested in what some men shall not do, in order to free other men from interference. But many jural laws are positive, as when a law requires men of a certain category to pay taxes or enter the military service.

It is sometimes said that a scientific law is obeyed invariably, while a jural law, depending on choice, is obeyed only approximately. But this distinction is not strictly valid. Nothing in nature is ever exactly what science conceives it to be. There is always some discrepancy between the law and the obedience; and both the scientist and the jurist try to reduce this discrepancy to a minimum. The scientist seeks a law which is as exactly as possible obeyed; and the jurist seeks to make beings obey the law as exactly as possible. The difference is one of degree, the jurist being less disturbed by individual deviations. Neither can predict with certainty; the scientist demands a higher probability.

Since the jural law is obeyed by choice, the jurist is concerned with inducements that move the will. These are called sanctions. He seeks to cause men to obey a given law, and therefore re-educates them, reasons with them, persuades them or makes threats and promises. He invokes the support of beings whom men are inclined to obey.

Jural law is thus associated in the human mind with the idea of a lawgiver. It speaks in the imperative voice and with an intonation of command. Even when the content of law is analyzed in its own terms, there is a lingering echo of some respected personal authority, whether God, or ruler, or parent, or some spokesman of tradition and public opinion, or the nearest policeman carrying his club and badge of office. To separate the law from a being that "lays down the law" is not to deny that as a matter of fact laws *are* commanded; or that the association of the law with the prestige or power of a lawmaker inclines men to its obedience. But the essential meaning of law is independent of, and tends to be obscured by, such association. The Ten Commandments might still be laws even if they were not commanded; and God might have issued commands without creating laws.

A law which really exists is a law which is obeyed, as distinguished from a law which is merely formulated, recorded, hoped for, or commanded. Law of this kind is sometimes called "positive law." It is not always recognized that the only kind of law that exists is positive law. A "dead letter" is a law which has died; that is, ceased to exist. This does not imply, however, that real laws do not have values. They are put into practice—that is, exist—because they have values; and by the same token they are open to criticism, repeal, or amendment because of their failure to realize these values.

There are two values which are inherent in the nature of jural law. Both are social values; that is, values enjoyed by others and not merely by the individual who obeys the law. The first is the value of regularity. This is the value that jural law shares with scientific law. It is deemed a good thing for a man that his physical environment abides by laws. This enables him to predict the occurrence of physical events and to plan his life accordingly. It is also useful to men that their social environment should be regular. It is then possible to predict the behavior of one's fellow men, and so to make ready for their behavior in one's personal plans or engage with them in concerted plans.

But laws possess, together with government and economy, a moral value. The assumption that law has a moral content finds expression in the common association of law with right and justice. So intimately are these three ideas associated that in many European languages their names, *lex, jus, droit, recht,* are used interchangeably.

It is the purpose of law to create not only regularity but beneficent regularity; that is, regularity which prevents conflict and promotes co-operation. If a law did not serve this purpose at all, it would not have existed. The jurist would not have been interested in creating it. But existing law may serve this purpose more or less; or it may cease to serve it, owing to changed conditions; or it may fail to embrace all conflicts or possibilities. When jurists propose *new* laws, and discuss them on their merits, this is their guiding principle: Does the law in question adjust interests so that they can live and work together, with the maximum profit to all concerned?

Because jural law rests on moral premises, it shares with morality a certain independence of real existence. It is customary to speak of a law such as the Golden Rule as a "moral law," regardless of the extent to which it is obeyed.

What is meant can be correctly expressed only in hypothetical terms. A moral law is a generalization of behavior, which *if it were* obeyed *would be* beneficent; that is, prevent conflict and promote co-operation. It is a law that would be obeyed in a perfected society. The idea that what ought to be is fully embodied in the natural and human world—that things are constitutionally what it would be good for them to be—is contained in the doctrines of Creation, Providence, and "Natural Law." But to question this foreordained union of the good and the real does not abase the moral law. The if's, would-be's, and ought-to-be's of life, the goals unattained, the standards not complied with, the counsels of perfection, still retain their validity nonetheless. If this were not so, it would be meaningless to frame new international law in advance of its enactment and observance, and to present arguments in its support.

Open any standard treatise on the subject and you will find there recorded the corpus of presently existing international law. It consists of general rules governing human behavior between governments or between men living under different governments. This law exists because its observance can be confidently expected. It embraces such matters as the following: political independence and intervention; naturalization and the treatment of aliens; the use of the high seas, fishing rights, and the status of merchant vessels; the extradition of criminals; the acquisition of territory and the fixing of boundaries; the making, interpretation, and termination of treaties; the immunities of heads of state or of diplomatic agents; arbitration and courts of international justice; embargoes and blockades; the declaration and termination of war; instruments and methods of warfare on land and sea, including types of weapons and the practice of deceit; privateering; prize courts; treatment of prisoners and of sick and wounded; treatment of civilians in belligerent countries; contraband and the rights of intercourse and of private property in time of war; occupation of enemy territory; the conduct of neutrals.[1]

When this body of law is surveyed, its imperfections are clearly evident. At least half of it deals with war or with conditions arising out of war. This half of international law does not even attempt to prevent war, but only to regularize it, or to mitigate its evils. The other half does solve minor conflicts, and postpone major conflicts, but so long as it does not provide a solution of the problem of war its failure overshadows its success. It eases human relationships across national frontiers, and provides a framework for international intercourse, but it falls far short of attaining either peace or the maximum of co-operation.

International law is also imperfect in the degree of its realization. Some of it is little more than the expression of a pious hope. Much of it is too irregularly or intermittently observed to beget confidence and a sense of security. Even the laws of war have in recent years been flagrantly violated. The lawbreakers have developed a force which has failed only by a narrow margin to plunge the world into a worse anarchy than any which history records.

In his famous essay on *Eternal Peace,* Kant remarks that states pay lip service to international law, despite the fact that "their philosophically or diplomatically composed codes have not, nor could have, the slightest legal force, since the States as such stand under no common legal constraint." He then adds:

Yet the homage which every State thus renders—at least in words—to the conception of law still proves that there is to be found in man a higher and greater moral capacity, though it may slumber for a time; and it is evidently felt that this capacity will yet attain the mastery over the evil principle in him.[2]

Others, like Kant, have cast doubt on the existence of international law, owing to the absence of constraint; though many of them have failed to see, as Kant saw, that the content of international law is moral, and that the constraint required is a moral mastery over evil. There are many forms of such constraint and mastery; and among them that physical force which today receives the major emphasis is the least revealing of the fundamental purpose of law.

When we ridicule such international legalisms as the Kellogg-Briand Pact, we mean not that it did not have physical force behind it, but that it had *nothing* behind it except a few strokes of the pen. International law does not, it is true, become effective by being written down, or even by the signatures of chiefs of state. There are, however, many compelling forces short of physical force.

When a state is tempted for selfish reasons to break international law, it is deterred, in the first place, by fear—a fear of being generally outlawed. Like the state which breaks a treaty, it not only loses the special benefits of that particular law, but acquires the general reputation of untrustworthiness which disqualifies it for future compacts with the same or other nations. It forfeits the good opinion of neutral states, with which it may someday need to enter into legal relations. The lawbreaking nation is not only isolated, but feared. Its action is unpredictable. Being unrestrained by any binding agreement which respects the

rights of others, it is viewed with disfavor by the international community, as a potential disturber of the peace
whose lawbreaking may break out at any time and hurt the
innocent by-stander, and which cannot be allowed to remain at large. It incurs odium and disapproval; it loses
caste, as does the criminal in a national community, and is
called by the same uncomplimentary names.

This disapproval by the general international public
may reflect not only fear and prudence, but that disinterested respect for moral principles which exists in some degree in all nations, and which is felt even when their interests are not immediately involved. This "conscience of
mankind" is not only moral, but is also forceful. It acts as
a threat to those who transgress it. All nations hesitate to
offend it, and however wolflike at heart, try to cover their
lawlessness with a legal sheep's clothing. The conscience of
mankind is also imposed by each nation on itself, and cannot be violated without remorse.

As has already been pointed out, conscience needs to be
perpetually criticized and revised by reason, lest it cease to
serve its moral purpose. Reason reveals the rightness of the
law as serving the ends of harmony and co-operation, and
moves the will to obey the law because it is right.

The sanctions of international law so far enumerated
betray more or less plainly—in the inducements which they
offer to choice, and by which they constrain men to obey—
the law's moral function. There are certain other motives,
deep-rooted in human nature, which are not in themselves
moral, but which are indispensable adjuncts of law. The
first of these is habit, which inclines men to repeat what
they have already done. The second is imitation, which inclines men to repeat what other men have done. Habit and
imitation together compose custom. Custom gives perma-

nence to a lesson or an art once learned. It spares men the pains of contriving each separate action, and enables them to divert their attention to new problems.

Custom disposes men to regularity for its own sake; it inhibits irregularity merely because it is irregular. It is the strongest and most continuously effective of all the forces of human nature which confer on human life the benefits of regularity, and is thus the law's most faithful friend. It is chiefly to custom that men owe the predictability and the reliability of the human environment. Organized society and human institutions are unthinkable without it. But custom (as distinguished from conscience, with which it is commonly confused) is indifferent to morality. There are trivial and conventional customs such as ceremony and protocol which do not concern morality at all. There are wrong customs as well as right. Custom lends its strength to superstition, injustice, and inhumanity. It is sometimes more important, for good ends, to break it than to keep it.

It is evident that custom cannot now be invoked to support the reform and extension of international law. It is true that some right international law is customary; and that all international law, if it is to be generally observed, must become customary. But the international law which is now customary is largely a law of war, and insofar as this is the case, custom must be broken. And that new international law which is to replace or amplify the old has first to be supported by other sanctions before it can be repeated, and become a *new* old custom.

Hence the present importance for international law of the sanction of physical force. This sanction is not the first principle of law, but its last resort. Its use is evidence of lawlessness and not of law. But since the purpose of law is to substitute law for lawlessness, the suppression of lawlessness may come first in time even though it comes last in logic.

The beneficent effect for which a reasonable man is justified in obeying the law does not accrue to him or to any man unless the law is generally observed. He may understand that the general observance of law is a good thing, since it substitutes peace for war and co-operation for isolation; but he cannot make its observance general merely by observing it himself. The effect of such unilateral observance is to encourage and promote the selfishness of the less scrupulous. Nor can he count on other men's obeying the law from a like understanding of its good. All men have a capacity for such understanding, but unhappily, whether from original sin or from insufficient education, this capacity is often darkened by ignorance or outweighed by passion. The appeal to reason has its place, but it is not enough. The conscience of mankind is not enough, since nations, like individuals, may be shameless and defiant. Custom is not enough, for it permits of exceptions, which may be all the more dangerous for being exceptional.

Reason, public opinion, conscience, and custom leave a residuum of lawlessness; and this residual lawlessness has to be dealt with, because otherwise it creates uncertainty regarding the behavior of any man outside the circle of one's trusted friends. It has to be dealt with because even the *occasional* lawless man or act, whose appearance is unpredictable, requires all other men to be at all times on their guard, and thus deprives them of the benefits of law. It leads to reprisals. It becomes a focus of infection by which the whole society may descend to anarchy.

If a man is to observe the law, he may therefore reasonably demand the strongest possible guarantee of its general observance; not an absolute guarantee, which is impossible, but a stronger guarantee than that afforded by the sanctions already enumerated. He requires a sanction which will appeal to every man, or to the least common denominator of human motivation. So he unites with others to create and support a political instrument of overwhelming force which will inflict pain on the disobedient, or deprive them of things which everybody prizes, such as property, liberty, or life. The law, then, speaks in a language which every man understands, whatever the degree to which his moral or intellectual capacities are developed.

A New York newspaper recently contained a story with the following headlines: "RESTAURANTS BALK AT SAVING ON MEAT THREE DAYS A WEEK. Many Ignore Mayor's Plea for 'Conservation Monday,' serving Steaks and Roasts. THOSE WHO HEED IT IRKED. Spokesman Says Observance Must Be General or Plan Should Be Discarded." [3] The logic of the matter is contained in this example. The Mayor's law will work only provided all interested parties obey it. Otherwise those who obey it place themselves at a competitive disadvantage. Those who fail to obey it for reasons of the general good must be appealed to on lower grounds, by penalties imposed by the Mayor's power. They then obey it from fear, and not from respect for the purpose of the law.

This is what we mean when we say today that any organization designed for the purpose of security must have "teeth" in it. We mean that there are lawless nations in the world who cannot be counted upon to abide by the dictates of reason, conscience, or right custom, and who must be addressed in a more primitive language, such as showing the teeth. We mean that it is unreasonable to ask any nation to abide by international law if lawless nations are allowed to profit by their lawlessness at the expense of those who keep the law. We concede that there is in all nations, including ourselves, a potentiality of lawlessness which may break into lawlessness at some future time. We conclude that a force must be created which will, if necessary, impose pain, weakness, loss of life, property, or liberty on lawlessness whenever and wherever it shows its head; hoping that the lawless, anticipating such penalties, will abstain from lawlessness, so that the penalty will never need to be imposed—a word to the wise, we hope, will be sufficient.

Of the several sanctions by which men are constrained to obey the law, only the sanctions of reason and conscience reveal the full meaning of the law. Only when men's obedience proceeds from these sanctions does its motive coincide with the purpose of the law.

By reason and conscience are meant nothing mysterious, transcendental, or even rare. They participate in the decisions of everyday life. There is, for example, a traffic law which prescribes that motorists shall cross an intersection only on a green light. A man may obey it from habit, from fear of fine or imprisonment, from respect for the opinion of interested or disinterested by-standers, from fear of being struck by another vehicle, or from *reason and conscience;* that is, because he realizes that traffic rules, in preventing collisions and facilitating the flow of traffic, are good for all concerned, because he desires that good of all, and sees that this rule will serve the purpose. The obeyer of the law knows what law in general is for, and what this law in particular is for; and he is for what the law is for.

There are jurists who take a very different view, and maintain that the meaning of law lies in the penalty attached to its breach; in the suffering of those who reject it rather than in the benefits enjoyed by those who adopt it. It is as though one were to say that if laws were not broken, there would be no law; whereas precisely the opposite is true—insofar as law is broken it has not yet come to be, or has failed, and ceased to be. To say that a law is that the breaking of which is punished is a parody of the law, as though one were to say that education is what teachers keep you in after school for not getting.

The prudence of avoiding the penalty has nothing whatsoever to do with the wisdom of the law. If the observance of the law were not beneficent, there would be no excuse for the penalty; it would be an instrument of tyranny or a form of senseless brutality. If all law were criminal law, there would be no crimes. Suppose a situation in which the government issued an arbitrary edict and continually punished or threatened those who disobeyed; and another situation in which a beneficent law was universally observed in the absence of penalties. The first would then represent the minimum of law; the second would represent its maximum. In proportion as international law achieves its primary purpose, there will be no need of any dental accessories except for the purpose of assimilating its nutritive benefits.

The men and nations of our time engaged in making international law are making it as though there were no international law. There are, it is true, pieces of international law. But we propose to make much of this old law obsolete, and to add new law. Here we start with moral law; that is, with hypothetical law, which we believe *would* be good if it were observed. The first step is to frame such hypothetical law, and to discuss its moral merits. We confer with one another in private and in public throughout the length and breadth of every land. In such a situation attention is focused on those values of law which we hope by its observance to enjoy.

Having a high degree of unanimity on the evil of war and the wrong of aggressive war; recognizing that this wrong tends to bring all other wrongs in its train and to prevent their remedy; having learned from recent and painful experience that there are nations which, having committed this wrong, are disposed to commit it again; feeling, in short, the grave and urgent need of international peace and security—we hasten to invoke that last foolproof and wholesale sanction which we call the sanction of force. We propose to use arms, or economic blockades, because these will touch the motives of every nation, including the lawless. We propose that this force shall be so mighty and inexorable that the fear of it will be sufficient. We propose to make it so clear that every nation will take the hint.

We start with the forceful agencies already at hand; namely, the particular nations which will have won the war. We justify their use because we attribute to these nations a will which largely coincides with the purpose of international law. And we propose in time to create an international agency of enforcement in which the public interest of all nations shall be more explicitly separated from the private interest of any one nation, and in which no nation's proper name shall appear, even camouflaged as a "permanent member."

This process of enforcement we embrace within a proposed constitution of the world. We declare that enforcement itself shall be legal—which furnishes additional evidence that enforcement cannot be the ultimate sanction of law. Enforcement may induce obedience, but what shall induce enforcement? Here we must appeal to the deeper sanctions of reason and conscience. We build enforcement on what we already have of reason and conscience, and at the same time that we employ it we propose to reinforce and broaden its support. We know that we cannot afford to neglect any sanction, that we must create new customs, increase enlightenment and goodwill. International law requires every man's observance—and therefore world-wide custom, enlightenment, and goodwill. This more extensive requirement means that the long-range and more fundamental sanctions will take longer to create, and that the short-range sanctions will have to bear a correspondingly greater burden. These short-range sanctions will bear most of the burden against the present enemy, so long as he remains unconverted. While we are seeking to re-create the minds of all mankind, we must deal with them as they are—high and low, good, bad, and indifferent—for we cannot wait, lest we be given no opportunity to do the re-creating. Furthermore, the sanction of force, though it is primarily designed to induce a present obedience, will contribute to this re-creating; for it will beget a habit of obedience, and nations, like individuals, may learn to prize an obedience which was first induced only by fear of a more unpleasant alternative.

What are those benefits for which international law will be prized by those who are compelled to live under it, and for the sake of which it is to be created and enforced? They are broadly the same as the benefits of all law extended more widely. Law follows morality across national frontiers and wide distances to embrace and benefit the lives of all men. A Nazi-minded jurist named Schmitt is quoted as saying, "Law is what is useful to German people. Law is what der Führer says." [4] International law is useful for *all* people. It is not what anybody says, but a **universal** order which *everybody* enjoys.

In Kant, again, we find the clearest understanding of the matter—both the disease and the remedy:

Human nature appears nowhere less amiable than in the relation of whole nations to each other. No State is for a moment secure against another in its independence or its possessions. The will to subdue each other or to reduce their power is always rampant; and the equipment for defense, which often makes peace even more oppressive and more destructive of internal prosperity than war, can never be relaxed. Against such evils there is no possible remedy but a system of international right founded upon public laws conjoined with power, to which every State must submit,—according to the analogy of the civil or political right of individuals in any one State. For a lasting universal peace on the basis of the so-called balance of power in Europe is a mere chimera. It is like the house described by Swift, which was built by an architect so perfectly in accordance with all the laws of equilibrium that when a sparrow lighted upon it it immediately fell.[5]

The best way to understand why we have law is to experience or imagine anarchy. Anarchy is that state of affairs in which you don't know what is going to happen next and fear the worst; and in which you *prepare for the worst,* which preparation is itself next to the worst. International law yields first, then, the benefit of regularity, which enables one nation to predict the behavior of other nations and to lay its plans accordingly. It stabilizes that total and world-wide social environment to which men must now learn to adapt themselves. The greater part of life will remain free from its regulation, consisting of those parts which are regulated by domestic or national law, and of those spontaneities and unique experiences which cannot and should not be legally regulated at all. Irregularity will then flourish and abound within a broad framework of regularity.

But what kind of regularity? What shall be the content, as distinguished from the form, of international law? In the first place, the new international law will eliminate conflict where it has hitherto occurred on the largest scale and with the most ruinous consequences. It is designed to prevent war—not, as in the past, to legalize it, but to make it illegal.[6] The use of violence for the settlement of disputes will then remain only as a last resort, taken from the disputing parties and reserved for some disinterested agency. All other resorts to violence, whether by arms or by economic pressures, will then become illegal acts, to be prevented, deterred, or punished. The totalitarian aggressors will have become the first criminals under this new conception; and their treatment is inspired by the hope that they may be the last. At the same time positive procedures for harmonizing international interests, procedures such as negotiation, arbitration, adjudication, or international controls, will be given the form of law; and their "must" will be the positive corollary of the "must-not" addressed to war.

Second, co-operation. The prohibition of war and the compulsion to employ other methods of settlement will enable mankind to live together. They may then work together and enjoy severally the goods which only their combined efforts and resources make possible, or which they can achieve at less cost by combination than singly. Public health, postal and cable services, the charting of the high seas, codes of navigation by sea or air, stable monetary exchange, global commerce, and the world-wide interchange of cultural creations can only be achieved by common action regularized by international law.

How far such legalized co-operation shall be carried can only be determined by experience, and permits of widely divergent opinion. This is, on a wider scale, precisely the same question that already divides opinion within each society. How much of life shall be collectivized and made a law for all, and how much shall be left to narrower units engaged in friendly competition? There is no general answer to this question, and the familiar arguments pro and con need not here be rehearsed. There is only one generalization which it is safe to make; namely, that competition shall be friendly—that competing units while pressing their narrower claims shall thereby serve the general good. Whenever international dealings are destructive, international law will prohibit; whenever they are clearly constructive of benefits to all mankind, international law will permit, facilitate, and protect—with due regard to the dangers and difficulties that beset the use of legal agencies on so vast a scale. However cautious and restrained in practice, it is the clear purpose of international law not only to render nations mutually noninjurious and safe, but to implement that greatest good of all nations and of all mankind which is the moral end.

The beneficence of law is commonly stated in terms of "rights." What is a "right," and how does international law affect its meaning? The understanding of the matter begins, and also ends, with individual rights. A right is a bounded sphere within which interests enjoy the protection of organized society. It expresses the primary fact that every interest is somebody's interest, and that its fulfillment requires that the somebody in question shall be enabled to carry on the activities which his interest dictates. Thus there is a right to private property primarily because there are persons who desire to possess material objects for their exclusive use. The right defines the limits within which this desire may have free play.

A right implies a duty as well as a privilege, because it leaves room for the enjoyment of like privileges by other individuals animated by the same or by a different interest. A boundary has two sides, and the right not only concedes to the individual what lies within the boundary, but prohibits him from trespassing beyond—it is affirmative within bounds, restrictive out of bounds. Thus the exclusive possession of material objects by one individual must be consistent with a similar exclusive possession and use of material objects by others. The individual may insist on his own right of property, but only provided he at the same time respects the property of others. Rights are, in short, reciprocal.

A right is protected by organized society; that is, its exercise by one individual is ensured by some public agency against interference by other individuals, as when the property right is ensured by the prevention of theft. The individual is thus not only allotted a sphere within which he may affirm his interest, but is relieved of the necessity of guarding its frontiers.

The new international outlook touches the question of rights at several points. First, there is a shift of emphasis from the permissive and prohibitive aspect of rights to their implementation. It is a noteworthy fact that in the Soviet constitution rights are not only allowed but *serviced,* as when the right of assembly is promoted by providing places of assembly, and national cultural rights by assisting in the cultivation of local languages and folkways.

Similarly, in Soviet Russia the rights of the press are conceived to embrace "the supply of toilers and their organizations with paper printing offices, buildings, communications and other commodities." [7]

The right of education, which is now universally recognized, implies educational facilities. It is not sufficient to prevent interference; it is necessary also to provide schools. Similarly, the right to life implies the provision of food and not merely the prohibition of homicide; the right to health implies the provision of medical care; the right to work implies the providing of jobs; * the right of leisure implies vacations and the means of recreation. The list of rights being no longer limited to rights which can be enjoyed by the unaided individual grows longer and longer. A recent *Statement of Essential Human Rights,* drafted by a committee of the American Law Institute, enumerates eighteen freedoms, of which seven, clearly recognized in from seven to forty countries, explicitly require that the state shall "maintain," "provide," or "assure" facilities, or "take measures," to make the freedoms effective. [8] When a colony or dependency is said to have a right to self-government, the statement is taken to imply that its people shall not be merely *allowed* to govern themselves and cast adrift, but that they shall be helped to their feet, loaned capital and the services of experts, and otherwise enabled to exercise and enjoy their independence. There is thus a growing tendency to emphasize the positive as well as the

* Thus the Murray Full Employment Bill, S.380, introduced on January 22, 1945, contained the following provision: "All Americans able to work and seeking work have the right to useful, remunerative, regular, and full-time employment, and it is the policy of the United States to assure the existence at all times of sufficient employment opportunities to enable all Americans who have finished their schooling . . . freely to exercise this right." All parties seem at present to be agreed on the right, differing only as to the point at which the public authorities shall intervene.

negative aspect of rights; or to charge organized society, whether national or international, with the duty of enabling and not merely allowing.

There is no doubt of the tendency. There is also no doubt of the merits of the question. The purpose of right, like the purpose of any form of social organization, is to promote the interests of the members of society. Its gift of freedom is empty if its members are unable to use it. The only valid reason for its withholding benefits from its members is that those benefits can sometimes be obtained more abundantly by other means—as, for example, by their own efforts; in which case, however, organized society is bound to facilitate those efforts, and be prepared to supplement them if necessary. The only reason for its not giving is lest by giving too much it should have nothing to give, or lest by promising too much it should be unable to keep its promises. How far such reasons are valid in any given case is a matter of expediency and not of principle.

International law, like all law, is a guarantor of rights. It is an additional guarantor of those individual rights, old and new, whose claims have been amplified by a heightened sense of the obligations of society to its members. It extends those rights to all men, at the same time that it multiplies their number, and interprets them more generously. This is the clear meaning of the statements of principle which have been affirmed, reaffirmed, and unitedly affirmed by the statesmen and moral leaders of the United Nations. The evidence of this is in the rights which are listed, and are capable of being exercised only by individuals; and in the frequent use of such terms as "people," "men," and "human personality" as though to guard against any other than an individualistic interpretation.[9]

Individual rights are called "human rights" when they are rights common to all men. The Roman jurists, who had to adjudicate the relations of men of diverse peoples, each with its own peculiar legal system and tradition, conceived of a law which applied to man as man, or to people as simply people. This they called *jus gentium*.[10] It was a law of which a man of any people might rightly claim the benefits, and which rested upon the universal opinion of mankind. When the rights of individuals are thus conceived, they may be called international rights—meaning individual rights which are international in their application and in their sanction.

International rights have, however, a second meaning, commonly confused with the first. They may be taken to mean the rights of a nation in relation to other nations. Similarly, international law may be taken to mean the law between nations, of which states rather than individuals are the subjects and the beneficiaries. A contemporary authority says:

The persons of international law, or the subjects in whom inhere the rights and obligations defined by the law, are the states or nations recognized as belonging to the international community. . . . By contrast with the natural persons who form the subjects of municipal law, the persons of international law are corporate juristic bodies possessing a unity or moral personality by reason of certain bonds that hold their individual members together.[11]

That politically organized societies may be said in their collective capacity, or through their governments, to exercise certain peculiar functions, cannot be denied. A nation-state occupies a portion of the earth's surface, possesses a total wealth or income, and makes war and peace; and these things are not done by individuals. You or I, for example, cannot make war on Hirohito, but the United States can and does make war on Japan. By virtue of the exercise of these functions a state possesses certain rights in relation to other states. When two states make a treaty, as only states can, each has a right to the fulfillment of its terms, and in that sense may be said to possess a moral personality; precisely as a business corporation, having through its directors made a contract, has an obligation to keep it, and a right to enjoy its profits.

There are those who say that moral personality of the state is more real, of greater dignity, than that of the member; and that the member shines in its reflected glory. According to this view the member has no rights of his own, but only borrowed rights. There are those, on the other hand, who reverse these roles, and say that the corporate person has no rights save as the aggregate or agent of the rights of its personal members. Those who have spoken for the United Nations have taken this second view—not for reasons of metaphysics, but because it is the traditional view in democratic countries, or because it seems to them to be the plain common sense of the matter.

Taking this second view, the expression "national rights" has two meanings. It means the rights of the individual members of one nation when these are set over against the rights of the individual members of other nations; or it means the rights of individuals when these are claimed and dispensed by their government, dealing with other governments. In both meanings national rights are rights of individuals *between* nations; and are, like all rights, reciprocally limited. A nation which existed alone in the world would have no rights. A nation which accepted no restraint upon its action would have no rights. A claim of rights must be based upon a system of rights. The expression "sovereign rights," if "sovereign" means unrestricted use of power against other nations, is a contradiction in terms.*

We hear much of sovereign rights; we also hear of sovereign equality. It is quite clear that this does not mean equality of power, though nations sometimes *behave* as though it did. It is clear that it does not mean equality in virtue, though all nations would like to *think* it did. It does not, and ought not, to mean political equality; that is, equal influence in the determination of international policy. It does not mean equality in anything except sovereignty. And it means equality of sovereignty only in a special sense. It does not mean an equal degree of sovereignty possessed by each national government over its own people. If some nations exercised an undisputed sovereignty at home and others were weakened by internal dissension, they would still be equal in sovereignty in the special sense here intended; namely, equality before the law.[12]

Every law is stated in general terms and is applicable to all particulars which qualify under the general, regardless of other differences. A tax law applies to a class of men who satisfy certain conditions of residence and property; and it applies to them equally—that is, without discrimination. Taxpayers who are equal in respect of their obligations to pay taxes are unequal in other respects, as, for example, the amount of their tax, their right to vote or to serve on juries, and their obligation to military service. Similarly, when international law defines the rights

* Cf. also above, Chapter III, page 93.

or obligations of social groups having their own governments—such as their right to exclude others from their
territory, or their obligation to respect the territory of
others—then this law is said to apply to them equally. They
are equal in respect of rights and obligations that *go with*
sovereignty, regardless of size, wealth, age, military power,
or geographical location.*

Equality before the law holds of all law. There is,
however, a difference in the breadth of application, and
therefore in the extent of its equalizing effect. A law
which applies to men as residents of a certain country
has a broader equalizing effect than a law which applies
only to its citizens; and a law which applies to men as men
has a universally equalizing effect. Sovereign rights equalize all nations having their own governments, but not
other nations, such as the Jewish nation—if it be a nation;
or other groups, such as Australian aborigines, which are
not nations. Sovereign rights thus create inequalities as
well as equalities. There is also a difference in the extent
to which laws embrace the interests of the men to which
they apply. All laws equalize some men in some respects;
some laws equalize some men in all respects; some laws
equalize all men in some respects; only moral law equalizes
all men in all respects.

If law is to take effect and confer its appropriate benefits,
it must be known to those who are required to obey it
and privileged to claim it. It must be formulated, recorded, and promulgated. But there is a gap between the
law and the concrete act, and courts are created to fill this

---

* Whether a society does or does not have a right to a sovereign government is another question altogether—namely, the question of "self-
determination" already discussed above.

gap. There are, no doubt, some cases in which the court has only to compare the act with the law and declare it legal or illegal. But this clerical job is a small part of the judge's function, and makes no demands upon the judge's special attributes.

The law does not apply directly to the concrete act, because it does not take account of special circumstances. It does not take account of new situations which the original framers of the law could not predict. One law, furthermore, does not always take account of other law. A concrete act must be either legal or illegal. It cannot be left indeterminate, and it cannot be both legal and illegal— legal under one law and illegal under another. A juristic system therefore requires an agency, called a court, which has to interpret the law and judge its consistency.

In exercising its functions the court makes law. For the law exists in its concrete legalities and illegalities and not in its abstractness. The law *is* what it *means* under specific circumstances and as part of the total legal system. The court, faced with concrete situations, alive to the human relations which the law is designed to render harmonious and co-operating, and being disinterested in its approach, renders the sort of judgments in which the purpose of law is revealed and in which its beneficence is most closely approximated. The court contributes largely to making the law what the law is, and it may contribute more wisely than the jurist by whom the law is formulated, or the statesman by whom it is enacted.

The judge is not, however, free to make the law what he would like it to be. He starts with the abstract law and has to remain faithful to it so far as it goes. He has to be guided by the framer's intent; he has to follow the path defined by previous decisions, lest the purpose of regularity be defeated. Without continuity and stability man would lack that guarantee of future expectations which is a condition of long-range and organized plans. A law whose interpretation changed every time it was adjudicated would be indistinguishable from anarchy.

All of these considerations apply, with changes of emphasis, to international courts, which are an indispensable adjunct of international law. The present is largely a phase of formulation and declaration. But as rapidly as international law is adopted, the matters to which it refers will become, as we say, "justiciable." An international court will interpret international law and determine the legality or illegality of the concrete acts of nations relatively to other nations, or of nationals relatively to other nationals. Whether there shall be a resort to international courts by individuals or only by governments is a procedural question which has yet to be answered. In any case, the role of the international court will in the near future be peculiarly creative because of the relatively large amount of new law whose meaning has yet to be clarified and applied.

As the world here and there emerges out of war into peace there arises a demand for "order," as the first condition of political, economic, or social restoration. The difficulty to which this demand gives rise is highly instructive. There is an issue between the orderly and the disorderly, and the pacifying force of the United Nations takes the side of order. But the nature of the order, and the benefits which it yields, depend on the law which the disorderly are asked to obey. The disorderly may resist not because they prefer disorder, but because they desire a better law than that law under which they have already lived. There are thus two issues: order versus disorder; new law versus old law. The exponents of order tend to take the side of old law, as being the law to which the people are accustomed and which can therefore be most promptly carried into effect; or as being the law of the occupying authorities, and which they have both the inclination and the power to enforce. It is well in this connection to recall that the intervention of the monarchical states against the French Revolution was justified as a prevention of anarchy.[13] Those who are called disorderly are, then, those who wish to take advantage of the present fluidity to create a better law of their own making, having acquired a revolutionary temper during the period of struggle, and a sense of merit by virtue of hardships endured.

There is no easy solution of this tragic dilemma, but it is something to clarify the principles by which a right solution may be governed. Law cannot be razed to the ground and rebuilt, because men have to live in a legal order during the process. On the other hand, law is not merely order; it is beneficent order. Stability is not the same thing as justice. Law, like medicine, may need to be shaken before using if it is to yield its curative effects. A state of affairs in which all parties obey the law may represent the failure and not the success of law. For over and above the value of regularity, law is designed to serve the interests of those who obey it—to serve them generously and to serve them all. If men are asked to obey for the sake of regularity a law they deem bad, then they must be convinced that the claims of justice and humanity are fully recognized and that their fuller achievement will not be too long postponed.

CHAPTER FIVE

World Economy

THE name "household" is given to a family considered as living together and as supplying their several needs, such as food, clothing, and shelter, out of a common fund of labor and possessions. Economy, in its original meaning, is the art of managing this domestic affair. From this primitive and relatively simple form, economy has been extended to larger social units until today we think of a family of all mankind keeping house together on the earth. Whatever the size of the household and the complexity of its needs, the art of management remains essentially the same; namely, to provide for needs by an organization of resources. And the aim is the same—to provide for needs as satisfactorily as possible, and at the least cost; that is to say, as "economically" as possible.

Both of these aims—the aim of maximum satisfaction and the aim of minimum cost—are essential to the meaning of an economy, and they contribute criteria by which an economy is to be judged a successful or sound economy. The first step in the analysis is to see how the second grows out of the first.

Human interests are seated in physical organisms and operate in a common physical environment. Sooner or later, and in some degree, they come into competition with one another for the use of this environment. Certain human interests are in principle nonacquisitive. They do not require the consumption or exclusive use of their objects, but may enjoy these in common with other interests, as when two or more persons delight in the same sunset, wonder at the same mystery, or seek an explanation of the same natural events. But even these interests tend to become acquisitive, in their means if not in their ends, as when two spectators compete for the use of the same point of observation, or two scientific expeditions for the exploration of the same area. And even if this did not occur, there would still remain a rivalry within each person for the use of the same organism.

Out of this situation, in which interests compete for the use of the same resources, there arises the economic problem of meeting the needs of one interest with the least deprivation to others' interests. The appeasement of its hunger, for example, requires that an organism shall seek out a suitable object—an edible object. It must employ its body for the purpose, and most forgo sleep, love-making, fighting, and other satisfactions that require the exclusive use of the same body. A solution is found in the adoption of a schedule by which the use of the body is allocated to the several interests at different times. This arrangement happily coincides with the periodic nature of the appetites themselves, so that their postponement is often a gain rather than a loss.

The same solution is sometimes applicable to the rivalry between one organism and another—when they cannot use the same external object at the same time, they can use it in rotation. But, unhappily, the first use is commonly the last. In order that hunger shall be appeased its edible object has to be eaten; that is, used up. One organism may seize the object, and pre-empt it at the cost of other hungers. This is the economy of plunder. But while this promises to satisfy the need of the predatory organism at little cost, it does not satisfy the second organism at all. The plundered organism will therefore resist, with the result that the object may be destroyed and both organisms may destroy one another; or they may be so preoccupied with the struggle that they cannot use the object. Thus plunder tends to a minimum of satisfaction and a maximum of cost. It so palpably fails to solve the economic problem that it were better considered no economy at all.

The simplest form of constructive or provident economy is the arrangement by which the objective is divided. It may happen that the competing needs are abundantly satisfied by a *portion* of the object, as, for example, by portions of an area of land where there is room for all. More often, however, the method of division tends to defeat the aim of the satisfaction of the need. Half a loaf is better than no bread, but it may be insufficient. The next step in the solution of the problem is to produce more bread, so that there shall be enough to go around. And production serves its purpose of satisfying needs only when it is *passed around;* that is, distributed.

Meanwhile, however, a new principle has appeared; namely, the principle of division of labor. Production and distribution cost time and effort, and if these are to be least costly they must be apportioned, and compensated by wages; that is, by a share of the product. There is a qualitative as well as a quantitative division of labor. Some men are more apt for one kind of labor and others for other kinds of labor, and some kinds of labor are in themselves repaying to him who labors. Production and distribution will then be least costly when they are divided by habit and inclination, as well as by amount of time and

effort. But the division of labor is not only relatively costless; it is also relatively fruitful, and thus serves the aim
of the maximum satisfaction of need. What men can
achieve by collaboration is far greater than the sum of
what they can achieve separately; not only because of the
greater force created, but because of the interadjustment
of diverse skills and forms of specialization. Production, as
distinguished from a hand-to-mouth economy, requires
tools, and a fund from which labor can be sustained before
its products are ready for consumption. These means of
production are called "capital," which may be provided by
nature or from a portion set aside, or "saved," from past
production.

The next step is exchange. If each of two men has in
excess what the other lacks, their needs can be met most
economically by exchanging what they have in excess.
This arrangement may be completely costless, as when each
party to the exchange gets what he needs and gives only
what he does not need. The same principle applies, however, when each party gains more than he loses, or gives
up what he needs less for what he needs more. The principle is capable of extension from a bilateral to a multilateral form in which the first party can obtain by profitable exchange with a third party what he can then
profitably exchange with the second party. It is capable of
being extended to all the interests of all the persons in a
community, so that everybody has something to give and
something to get; and so that every object for which there
is a demand is exchangeable for every other in a standard
ratio represented by its "price."

The technical problems and mechanisms which arise in
a highly developed economy need not concern us, since
they introduce no departure from the basic ideas here set

forth. These ideas apply to all economies, great and small, and to economies of every type.

It should now be apparent that economy is a moral solution of a moral problem. The problem is a problem of conflict and helplessness, and the solution is a solution by harmony and co-operation. The minimum economy substitutes constructive for destructive methods of adjusting the conflict of needs. And even in the minimum economy there is some recognition of the claims of all parties to the transaction. As economy develops, it satisfies needs more abundantly and pays increasing tribute to the rights of all men to a just share of its benefits.

The moral standard by which an economy is justified receives its most striking and timely illustration from an examination of that type of economy which is known as the private-profit economy or laissez-faire capitalism. The name "laissez-faire," like so many names, calls attention to the accident rather than the essence. It refers to the absence or minimum of control by government, and means that an economy will best serve society if it is allowed to be an economy pure and simple, in which the so-called economic forces are allowed comparatively free play. It has never meant, nor can it ever mean, that there should be no control of economy by government and law; for its operation is dependent on a body of laws which regulate property, contract, corporations, money, and many other items of the economic process.

This system is called "capitalism" not because it employs capital—all production requires capital. It is sometimes called the system of "private property," but this is not an adequate criterion, because all economies imply *some* private property. Consumption is private, and most consumption requires that the object consumed shall be the property of him who consumes it—at least at the moment of consumption. Nor does it suffice to describe the system in terms of private profit, since all economies are privately profitable.

The distinguishing feature of the system which is called by these various names is a combination of the ideas which they severally connote. It is the system in which capital is private property. It is the system in which the economic good of society—the most abundant satisfaction of everybody's needs, at the least cost to all concerned—is supposed to result from the relatively unhampered operation of the motive of private profit. All the essential economic functions—production, distribution, labor, wages, capital, exchange—are entrusted to the interaction between one gainfulness and another. When each party seeks, without resort to violence, to give up as little as possible in return for getting as much as possible, then all will enjoy the greatest possible margin of getting over giving up.

Laissez-faire capitalism is thus a mechanism or technique of selfishness justified by its self-transcending consequences. Selfishness, it is claimed, becomes generally beneficent when one selfishness is pitted against another. The system is operated *for* the public good; but the operatives are baited *by* their private good. The basic philosophy is to be found not in the shrewd calculations of each selfish interest but in the disinterested approval of its social good. The economic transaction commends itself to the buyer or seller, the lender or borrower, the employer or worker, by what he himself gets out of it, while at the same time it commends itself to the citizen, the moralist, the disinterested statesman, or the public, by what *everybody* gets out of it. There is a double pay-off.

ONE WORLD IN THE MAKING

ONE WORLD IN THE MAKING

The moral standard by which laissez-faire capitalism is judged appears in the professions of its own exponents—from Adam Smith to the American businessman of 1945. In his *Wealth of Nations* Adam Smith appealed to the principle of calculating selfishness; but this calculating selfishness, under the name of prudence, was justified on higher grounds in his *Theory of Moral Sentiments*. The American businessman, as represented by the National Association of Manufacturers, puts it as follows: "We believe the economic system which is commonly called free enterprise will provide the highest standard of living for all people." [1]

No American businessman justifies his creed on the ground that it will improve his own standard of living, or even that of his immediate friends and neighbors, but that of everybody. The argument is familiar. When selfishness competes with selfishness, the competitors bid against one another in service to the consumers on whose custom their profit depends. Success depends on providing what people want, and at a lower price than others offer. The goods produced are the goods demanded, and they tend to find their way to those who demand them. Competition puts a premium on thrift, invention, and efficiency. The hope of great private gains induces a willingness to take great risks, and benefits the public through the investment of savings in new forms of enterprise. Finally, the system makes, or leaves, men free. They can choose their occupations; and if they bind themselves by contracts, they do so of their own will.

The exponent of laissez-faire capitalism thus commits himself to a fundamental moral standard, and he cannot complain if his own standard is used to correct, supplement, or even condemn laissez-faire capitalism. This can-

dor and consistency is illustrated by the president of the
United States Chamber of Commerce, who has said:

The capitalism of complete laissez-faire, which thrived on
low wages and maximum profits for minimum turnover,
which rejected collective bargaining and fought against justified public regulation of the competitive process, is a thing of
the past. Those who would turn back the clock of history in
this respect are as unrealistic in their way as the addle-brained
paper planners of an economic solution.[2]

But the recognition of its moral liabilities began on the
day that laissez-faire capitalism was born. The Christian
conscience had always protested against usury, low wages,
and other forms of exploitation in which a man took advantage of his neighbor's extremity. The so-called Industrial Revolution seemed to aggravate rather than remedy
these evils. It was seen that if left to itself the new system
might lower the standard of living of large numbers of
people, tempt women and children to excessive hours of
labor, and create congested masses of workers living in
dependence on the concentrated power of those who controlled their means of livelihood. The rich drove hard
bargains; the poor had little choice. In England these
evils disturbed social reformers like Robert Owen, one
of the early leaders of the trade-union movement and the
statesmen who initiated factory legislation. This duty to
intervene *against* laissez-faire capitalism in behalf of that
same general good which is invoked in its support has
never been disputed, and such intervention has steadily
increased and is still increasing; until minimum wages,
health, education, equal opportunity, insurance against
disability, and the power of labor through organization to
assert its claims to a fair share of the benefits of the econ-

omy are generally endorsed by the social conscience and incorporated into public policy.

As laissez-faire capitalism developed, the emphasis shifted from this external humanitarian protest to an analysis of the system itself. It was claimed that laissez-faire capitalism contained the germs of its own destruction, that it broke down, and ceased to work; that is, ceased for internal reasons to yield its promised benefits. The acme of competitive success is not to do more business than the competitor, but to put him out of business altogether. Competition tends to monopoly, and therefore to noncompetition. Monopoly tends to restriction of output in order to raise prices. It resists technological change—so far as merely competitive success is concerned it is not necessary to employ improved techniques; it is sometimes simpler to deprive others of their use. Labor being treated as a cost of production, the tendency is to depress wages, and so to reduce the purchasing power of consumers, most of whom are workers. When production outruns purchasing power, plants are closed and labor is denied employment altogether. The thrifty who have accumulated capital are not compelled to take risks, but are disposed to play safe and lend to the government at a low and guaranteed rate of interest; and when private capital is idle, there is no private enterprise. As a result of these and other causes inherent in the dynamics of the system itself there is a tendency to business cycles and to periodic crises in which the whole life of the community is paralyzed and men are in more desperate straits than they ever suffered in the most primitive pastoral or agricultural economies.

The heart of the indictment, whether humanitarian or technical, lies in the cumulative inequality of bargaining power. Taking advantage of this inequality is called "exploitation." Each party to exchange gets something he needs *more* in exchange for something that he needs *less*, and thus betters his situation. But according to the principle of "diminishing utility," the extent to which a man *needs* what he has depends on how *much* he has. He may have so little as to need *everything* he has, and may be compelled to give up what he badly needs for what he needs more desperately, as when he is compelled to give his money for his life. A second party may have a surplus that he does not need at all, or only for some extravagant luxury. The conception of price conceals this inequality, since two objects exchanged, whatever their place in each party's order of need, are deemed to be of equal price. This is what price means—not the degree of need, but the ratio of exchange.

This inequality of bargaining power, in which something which one needs much is exchanged for something which somebody else needs *little or not at all*, is not rectified, but perpetuated or even aggravated, by the effects of each successive bargain. Those who have the initial advantage tend to improve it by their accumulated and consolidated gains. The rich grow richer and the poor grow poorer, until society tends to be divided into two classes: the plutocrats who can pay out of their abundance and not feel it, and the proletarian who has nothing to give except his body and his time, about which he feels very strongly.

Insofar as this is the case, the economy does not serve the moral purpose by which it is justified. The poor cannot be expected to take it lying down, unless in addition to their poverty they are also held in ignorance and superstition. They will combine against the rich and sell their services more dearly. Or in the last analysis they may resort to violence, feeling that they have nothing to lose but their lives and having come to place little value on these.

Whether the solution lies in the reform of capitalism or in the substitution of some other and radically different system is not here in question. The point is that laissez-faire capitalism exists for society and not society for laissez-faire capitalism, or for the exclusive benefit of any class that may happen to benefit by it. The general good or moral purpose to which the advocates of laissez-faire capitalism themselves appeal in its behalf is entitled to a voice, and a voice to be heard above all other voices. It may speak in the name of religion or of social reform, or in the name of those who suffer from injustice. It expresses the conscience of men, their sympathy for poverty, illness, and frustration; it condemns the exploitation of the poor, the weak, and the helpless by the profit-seekers. It views the community as a whole, and finds it intolerable that certain groups of men should be the prey of others who control the sources and instruments of wealth. It speaks for the all-interest, and intervenes between man and man to prevent the *some-interest* from the abuse of its powers. In some degree, greater or less, it annuls the maxim that a man may "do as he likes with his own."

The aim being clear, the field is open to any economic device that will do the job, account being taken of the costs of change itself and the injustice of disappointing legitimate expectations growing out of the past. This view of the matter is, no doubt, felt to be "addle-pated," shocking, and even dangerous. It is about as shocking as the Ten Commandments, and considerably less dangerous than the Sermon on the Mount.

There is a trend to a planetary or global economy.[3] Technological changes, which have improved communication and transport, multiplied contacts throughout the world, and made them closer, have brought a corresponding expansion of economic relations. Man tends to do business with man whenever he can reach him, and man can now reach from anywhere to anywhere, provided only that both places are somewhere on the surface of the earth.

At the same time that men are enabled to strike bargains, transport goods, buy and sell, lend and borrow, from opposite parts of the earth, there is a tendency to expansion arising from the nature of the economic processes themselves. The methods of mass production—by conveyor belt and assembly line, by concentration of labor, capital, and research—look to world-wide markets. Manufacture, employing the advancing discoveries of industrial chemistry, draws from all parts of the globe its great diversity of rare minerals and other raw materials. Thus a modern telephone manufactured in the United States makes use of thirty-seven principal raw materials, drawn together from Mexico, Venezuela, Brazil, Bolivia, Argentina, Canada, Alaska, England, Ireland, France, Sweden, Germany, West Africa, Madagascar, Russia, India, China, the Philippine Islands, Australia, New Zealand, and the Netherlands East Indies. As has been noted, the modern American automobile contains 185 such elements, brought similarly from widely distributed localities.[4]

There is, it is true, another side of the picture. The present century has witnessed the spreading of industry to areas which were once looked to only as a source of raw materials. There has been a tendency to autarchy, or economic self-sufficiency; and there are evidences of what has been described as a "second industrial revolution," which "substitutes ubiquitous and unlimited elements of the in-organic world for the localized and scarce products of geo-logical and biological evolution. . . . The forces which oppose the economic integration of the world are unques-tionably gaining in strength." [5] But autarchy is primarily an effect of war rather than of economic forces themselves; the spread of industrialization to new areas requires the import of machinery and other capital goods from older industrial areas, and paves the way to exchange of manu-factured goods; and the "second industrial revolution" is as yet no more than a backward ripple on the surface of the first.[6]

There remains, however, the question whether a global economy is a good economy. An economy is not necessarily better because it is bigger. Dog can eat dog, whatever the size of the dogs. Every form of economy—from the no-econ-omy of plunder, through every degree of economic ex-ploitation, to an ideal economy in which all human needs receive their maximum satisfaction and their just due—is at least conceivable on a world-wide scale.

Those who do not thoughtlessly assume that the bigger is the better, identify global economy with some one of the benefits which they believe it will yield. They think of the global economy as the *peaceful economy,* which will pre-vent war from growing out of economic rivalry; or as the most *fruitful* economy, which will satisfy human needs most abundantly and with the least cost; or as the *free* economy, which by abolishing political barriers will per-mit economic forces to display their inherent beneficence; or as the *just* economy, which will yield to all men and all groups of men their rightful share of material goods; or as the *unified* economy, which will procure the maximum of economic efficiency through over-all organization.

These conceptions of world economy as the best economy are in some degree overlapping and in some degree inconsistent, but they provide a useful division of the topic, and of the merits of the question.

Economy, like politics and law, begins with the problem of conflict and seeks to prevent its breaking into violence. It is claimed for global economy that it solves this problem on a world-wide scale, and averts that most destructive form of conflict which is called war. Domestic economy prevents individuals from quarreling over material possessions by substituting a constructive reconciliation of their rival needs; global economy does the same as between one human family and another. It extends the solution to the dimensions of the problem: like problem, like solution.

Against the thesis that global economy prevents war it has been argued that the wars of the eighteenth and twentieth centuries followed eras of economic expansion. The extension of European trade to the Far East and the Americas in the sixteenth and seventeenth centuries brought the great commercial nations—England, the Netherlands, Spain, Portugal, and France—into conflict at their peripheries and made world wars of what might otherwise have been merely European wars. The rivalry for world markets and raw materials in the nineteenth century did not prevent, and is supposed to have promoted, the great world wars of the present era.

This proves, however, not that the economy does not prevent war, but that if it is to do so, it has to be *inserted at the point of conflict*. Two parties may go to war in order to secure for themselves the exclusive opportunity of peaceful trade with a third party. The remedy lies in constructive economic relations between the first and second parties.

The world-wide expansion of ruthlessly competing national economies is not a world economy, but only plunder on the grand scale. It illustrates the tragic fact that groups of men who have achieved peace within themselves become all the more destructive in their war on one another.

A world economy means, then, that all societies competing for material goods abandon the warring method of forcible seizure *all along the line,* and substitute the peaceful method of producing enough for all and distributing it justly by exchange.

Material possessions are not the only thing men quarrel about.[7] They quarrel for love, for power, for honor—for anything they prize. They may quarrel over material possessions not for themselves, but in order to possess the requisite materials for a war waged on some other ground, or to deprive some enemy of their use.[8] The fact remains, however, that a global economy would remove or diminish one of the major causes of war—providing, further, that it is the right kind of economy. For war is provoked not only by the absence of economy but also by slavery or exploitation. The impoverished, the desperate, and the resentful have no stake in their existing economy, and will be disposed to overthrow it and revert to plunder. They become the blind followers of ambitious demagogues, and look for compensation in a soldier's career; or they may be fired with zeal for some instant and radical reform. Such grievances and thwarted hopes existing anywhere create an instability that tends to spread from riot to revolution and from revolution to war. Whether economy conduces to war or to peace thus depends not only on its extension to world-wide proportions, but also on its justice.

Economy is a condition of peace, but peace is also a condition of economy. From fear of war nations resort to autarchy and so deny themselves the superior or cheaper commodities that they could import from abroad. A society geared to war must curtail the production of consumer goods and deny its members the material facilities of their preferred pursuits. Modern war puts a premium on long-range preparation, and to be powerful in war a nation must therefore remain perpetually on a war footing. The power economy contradicts the welfare economy.

The economic conditions of peace and the pacific conditions of economy are parts of one fact. The creation of a just world economy contributes to peace and to all the blessings of peace. The creation of peace is more than a negation of war; it fosters all the benefits of a provident economy—benefits justly enjoyed by all mankind and in terms of all their interests.

The world economy is sometimes conceived as the most fruitful economy, that is, the economy which serves the essential purpose of satisfying human needs most abundantly and at the least cost. According to the Book of Genesis, the earth was amply provisioned before God gave man dominion over it. This was why God, looking at his creation, pronounced it very good. There was plenty for everybody, and it was meant for everybody.

The idea of a natural plenty needing only to be apportioned to human needs still lingers; but it has been amended if not superseded by the idea of artificial plenty. "The fact is," says a recent writer, "that mankind now possesses the means of utilizing the rich resources of the earth so that every human being the world around may be supplied with the means of comfortable existence." [9] Mother Nature supplies the raw material; human labor and ingenuity supply the rest. By modernized economy on a world-wide scale there can still be plenty to satisfy the multiplied needs of a humanity that has generously obeyed the Creator's injunction to "be fruitful and multiply."

Ever since the incident of the little pigs, slaughtered to preserve their scarcity value, "the economy of abundance" has been, among Americans, a phrase to conjure with. The war economy has confirmed this faith. The amazing productive capacity of modern industry under the stimulus of war has proved to the satisfaction of most people that no one need lack the necessities of life, or even a modicum of luxury.

At the same time that this dream of plenty has seized the imagination of men, they have become more sensitively aware of the contrast between the dream and the reality. Someone has said: "It's one world all right, and so is a coconut one coconut. But an awful lot of both of them is husk." The husk of the earth comprises not only its unfertile parts but its undernourished inhabitants. Thus Asia, exclusive of Soviet Russia, contains 52 per cent of the earth's population, with a high rate of increase, but produces only 34 per cent of its cereals and a negligible percentage of its manufactures. In other words, a large fraction of mankind has neither sufficient food at home nor sufficient purchasing power to obtain it abroad. From the global standpoint this is a profound maladjustment which calls for an "equalizing" of the "earth's bounties." [10]

There is a dramatic contrast between the vastness of man's failure and the vastness of his hopes—both newly felt. This confession of failure widely acknowledged, and this sense of power widely claimed, have begotten in our day the purpose of an economic salvation that shall not only save men from present misery but raise them to heights of welfare never hitherto attained. This purpose is proclaimed by the privileged and the disinterested, as well as by the underprivileged, who, having heard good news, and been promised better things by rivals bidding for their support, will no longer accept their lot as hopeless.

It is dangerous to assume that an economy of war can be converted into an economy of peace. It is one thing to produce goods for the limited and definite ends of war, when the costs are not counted and when under the stress of emergency men are willing to submit to centralized controls; it is another thing to produce for the diversified ends of peace, when the piper has to be paid and when men feel entitled to press their conflicting interests. But these doubts do not affect the basic idea that the potential productivity of a modernized economy is sufficient to raise the minimum of human welfare above the level of destitution; and that a higher standard of living can be paid for by increased employment and purchasing power. No economic party denies this basic idea, whether it looks to free enterprise or to government. Associated with this idea is a resolve to adopt such economic measures as may be necessary to put it into practice.

No one denies that the way to increase human welfare throughout the world is to direct the efforts of all mankind consciously and methodically to that end. On one side of the equation, the needs, desires, and aspirations of all mankind; on the other side of the equation, the total resources of nature combined with the total resources of mankind—the same mankind. All men to help ourselves by concerted effort. All men to profit from the same fund of resources. All resources to be put to their most efficient use, measured in terms of human needs, and to their most economical use, measured in terms of human costs. Everything and everybody to be put to use in such manner as will add most and subtract least. All materials, all efforts, all skills, and all their geographical distributions so employed as will make the most of the fecundity of combination, division, and organization.

To those of its supporters who accept the classical theory of economics and its applications during the nineteenth century the world economy means the free economy; that is, economy delivered from political interference at the national frontiers as well as at home. Free trade abroad is conceived as the logical sequel to free enterprise at home.

The wars of the present century have created barriers between nation and nation which, while explicable in political terms, are "artificial" when judged by economic standards. The frontiers created by peace settlements at the close of the First World War encouraged nationalistic independence in defiance of economic interdependence. Autarchy arising from supposed military necessity lowered standards of living. In order to protect domestic interests, states erected tariff barriers and thus encouraged the creation of industries that were not economical. War and the preparation for war directed industry into unproductive channels, and subjected it to hampering controls. The obstacle of distance has already been removed. Down with the tariffs, off with the controls, and away with the restrictions. On with business, let economy be unconfined!

Such is the argument, and no one denies it a large measure of truth. But it is not the whole truth. While the removal of barriers would permit of trade on a wide scale, it is important not to confuse the benefits of economy with the space it covers, or with its mere internationality. If trade between two places is of mutual benefit to the people who reside there, and is prevented by their inaccessibility, then it is a good thing that modern technology should render them accessible; if the mutual benefit depends on speed, as in the exchange of perishable goods, then it is a good thing to have that speed increased. But it does not follow that an exchange between distant points is any better than exchange between near neighbors. It is true that if exchange is profitable between Hungarians on one side of the frontier and Czechs on the other side, then it is undesirable that it should be hindered; but it does not follow that exchange between Hungarians and Czechs is in itself better than exchange between Hungarians and Hungarians or between Czechs and Czechs. Trade should be freed from ownership of the territory with which one trades, and this would go far to deliver the world from the evils of economic imperialism, but this does not prove that trade between different territorial jurisdictions is any better than trade within the same. It would be possible within a global economy for Americans to do business with the inhabitants of New Guinea, but it might be more profitable for all concerned that they should do business with Maine and California. There should be world markets for the use of those who can profit by them, but world markets are not intrinsically superior to domestic markets. Mobility is desirable, but motion may or may not be desirable.

Whenever the term "freedom" is used, it should be closely scrutinized lest one succumb to its semantic spell. Whose freedom? Freedom to do what? Freedom with power, or freedom with impotence? Freedom used or freedom abused?

There are certain well-worn truths regarding freedom that must be kept in the forefront of the discussion. It is reasonable to suppose that those who advocate freedom are primarily concerned, and rightly concerned, with their own freedom or the freedom of others like them. When the demand for freedom comes from businessmen, it may therefore be assumed that the freedom intended is the freedom of the businessman to do business. But the freedom of business is not the only *kind* of freedom; and the freedom of one businessman or group is not the only *instance* of business freedom. There is, for example, the freedom of a big businessman and the freedom of a little businessman.

One freedom commonly competes with another freedom, so that its exercise by one man hampers its exercise by another. Ideal or right freedoms are reciprocally limiting, within some general system of freedom that is designed to provide a maximum freedom for all. Furthermore, freedom is proportional to the range of choice among alternatives, and is thus measured by knowledge of possibilities and fullness of opportunity. Effective freedom means capacity, and not merely permission, to do as one chooses. When all these considerations are taken into account, it is clear that a policy which may spell freedom to one man may spell compulsion to another; and that the prohibition of one man's freedom may be the only means of creating the other's freedom.

These same considerations apply to the freedom of nations. A nation's freedom to do business may have to be restricted in behalf of its other freedoms, cultural, political, or religious. One nation's freedom to press its economic advantages over a second may have to be denied or regulated in behalf of the freedom of that second. A merely permitted freedom of a nation, through noninterference, may mean nothing, owing to its ignorance or incapacity; the first step toward its effective freedom may have to be taken elsewhere, in the areas of education and welfare, or in associating freedom with power through political emancipation; and these steps may somewhere limit strictly economic freedoms. Economic freedom on the international level—the freedom of societies or groups—requires, then, a global system, which assists and does not merely refrain, and within which all national freedoms advance together.

Furthermore, the economic freedom of nations within a global framework may or may not enhance the economic freedom of their individual members. The fact is that individual freedom tends to be lost sight of through preoccupation with international trade. Freedom of competition at home may be suppressed for the sake of more effective competition abroad. The national conscience may not extend to its imperial perimeter, and may condone abroad abuses which it forbids at home; as when "respectable citizens" engage in the slave trade, or in rumrunning, or in the exploitation of defenseless natives. The international trader is concerned with deliveries and credits, and tends therefore to support whatever governments in other nations he can do business with, regardless of their internal economic policies.

Hence the solidarity of interest felt by labor throughout the world. The moral claims of labor do not rest upon its class interest merely, but on its representing those individuals and groups which feel that they are denied their due share of the benefits which the several national economies owe to their members. The International Labor Office, which has survived the collapse of the League of Nations, continues to proclaim the freedom of workers against the inordinate freedom of employers and owners of private capital. Workers believe that their freedom should be guaranteed for all nations and dependencies by treaties or agreements made by the United Nations; and that this freedom depends on public policy within each nation providing for regular employment under fair wages and reasonable conditions, improved standards of living, child welfare, collective bargaining, and insurance against disability, unemployment, and old age.[11] Similarly, the idea of "economic democracy" expresses the belief that a free economy, even on a world-wide scale, may result in an inequality of power so great as to make the many dependent on the few. Economic democracy, like organized labor, speaks for freedom against freedom, and invokes a just system of limited freedoms.

A global economy, even though it be created by economic freedom and defended in its name, does not, therefore, necessarily promote the general freedom; that is, effective freedom of choice for all nations and all men in all spheres of life. It is capable of the same abuses, and requires the same political or legal restriction, as laissez-faire capitalism in the domestic sphere. Free competition may be suppressed at home in the interest of more effective competition abroad. Nations cannot be allowed freedom of trade in slaves, white or black, or in noxious drugs. International monopolies arise from the same causes as domestic monopolies; in both cases the acme of successful competition is the elimination of the competitor. International monopoly leads to the same evils as domestic monopolies: limitation of output in order to maintain a high price level, resistance to invention and progress in order to protect vested interests, and the creation of excessive power in private hands. The power of international monopoly is proportionally greater than that of domestic monopoly, and may be used against the national interest as well as against the interests of individual consumers. The evil of the "cartel" does not lie in its unified control, but in the fact that this control is exercised irresponsibly by private individuals—who are not less private for belonging to several nations.

In short, if economic freedom is to be enjoyed to the maximum degree by all parties, national and individual, it does not suffice that the public authorities shall keep hands off. The original and most persistent threat to a private freedom is another private freedom; the public authorities are created in order to meet this threat. It is true that the public authority then constitutes a new threat to private freedom, but it would be folly from fear of public tyranny to revert to private tyranny and allow it to grow to new and global proportions.

It is the function of political and legal authority to define, implement, and protect those limited freedoms which are mutually consistent and harmonious. The way to correct its abuses is to use it, not to reject it. This authority alone is the responsible agent of all freedoms. If economic freedom is to be raised to the maximum throughout the world, there must be a corresponding political and legal authority which shall apportion freedoms, lest they destroy one another. If by freedom is meant everybody's freedom, then it is not promoted by denying power to its only effective champion.

If a world economy is the "best" economy, it must be a *just* economy; that is, an economy which dispenses its benefit to all, the claims of all men, groups, or nations being acknowledged equally or disinterestedly. There are those who believe that if an economy is free, its justice will take care of itself. Justice does not have to be *imposed* on economic forces, but is their by-product—"economic forces" being taken to signify the interaction of competing units each prompted by an enlightened regard for its own interest. On the global plane, this means that if a nation seeks its own welfare and prosperity, and does so intelligently, it will automatically promote the welfare and prosperity of mankind. This being granted, it is then possible to praise the global economy in terms of the maximum material good of all while appealing for its support in terms of the maximum material good of each. This equation between the economic good of all and the economic good of each is sometimes attributed to "intuition." Wishing to persuade his listeners to support a friendly policy toward Latin America, the geological broadcaster already quoted said:

> Enlightened selfishness may not be the most noble impulse to which to appeal, but it is the only one to which a great many people will respond. . . . Indeed, the moral conviction is itself based in part upon intuition that that is the kind of world in which men are most comfortable as well as most honorable. The more evidence we can amass to verify the correctness of that intuitive belief, the stronger and more widespread will be the allegiance to the noble idea.[12]

The president of the United States Chamber of Commerce has appealed for aid to devastated countries "in the name of decency or in the cause of self-interest." [13] The term "decency" lets the moral cat out of the bag. The cloak of enlightenment does not cover the nakedness of self-interest, even to the extent of decency—to say nothing of nobility.

It is an odd paradox that the scientist and the businessman should thus resort to intuition and dogma. A scrutiny of the facts of life discloses the inescapable fact that there is a collision between selfishness, however advanced and modernized, and that application of the Golden Rule which requires a man to be concerned with the prosperity of others equally with his own. The history of the Industrial Revolution affords overwhelming evidence that in proportion as the pursuit of private gain has been reinforced by science, experience, and the sharpening of men's competitive wits, it has proved necessary for conscience, religion, and the state to intervene against economic selfishness in behalf of justice and the general good. That the conduct dictated by self-interest and that dictated by disinterestedness coincide up to a certain point is highly important, since it diminishes the area in which public policy must restrict private liberties. In an ideal world self-interest and disinterestedness would no doubt coincide altogether. But in the actual world up to date they disagree and diverge beyond a certain point; which is precisely what is meant when this world is compared unfavorably with some other world, such as Paradise before the Fall, and the Heaven of the saints.

Since enlightened self-interest and justice do not invariably coincide, the promise that justice will always pay in terms of self-interest cannot be kept; and if you win a man's support by such a promise, you deceive him, and earn his future resentment. Meanwhile you have hindered rather than helped the course of moral progress; for instead of inclining men's hearts to justice, you have encouraged them to believe that they can remain selfish, and entrust justice to the natural order of things.

The essence of economic selfishness is the exploitation of a fellow man by taking advantage of his inferior bargaining power. If you are selfish, you press this advantage, hold it, and increase it. The fact that your bargain is cheap to you and costly to him does not disturb you. If he is so situated that you can buy his servitude out of your surplus, this does not disturb you. You acknowledge no obligation to view the matter from his point of view except when this enables you to get more out of him. If he is to get more out of you, that is his business and not yours; or the business of some higher agency which takes account of both, and which will always require some concession from each. This holds of the relations of individuals and groups within a society where the prosperity of the community as a whole requires concessions from every narrower prosperity. It holds of the relations among societies, where the prosperity of the world community must demand concessions from each national prosperity.

It is true that if you are an American businessman with a surplus to sell abroad, you will need customers and will desire that these shall be able to pay for what they buy. To that extent you will wish them well, and even encourage a rise in their standard of living in order that they may want, and pay for, your surplus more abundantly. If, however, they develop their own industries and supply their own wants, or if under the teaching of some ascetic religious leader they reduce their wants and go in for the simple life, you will view such changes with dismay and your visiting salesman will endeavor by what means he can to persuade them otherwise. Your better nature might lead you to say that they have the same right to their way of life that you have to yours; and that the best solution of the problem will be that disinterested solution which will take account of both your interest and theirs, even though it diminishes your profits, or requires you to go into some other form of business. But if you decided to prevent your customers' industrialization or religious regeneration, and could get away with it, there could be no complaint against you on the ground of enlightened selfishness.

If a highly developed national economy profits by the cheap labor of a more backward society, there would be no selfish good reason why the former should not use its power to prevent the latter from acquiring the means to improve its bargaining position, and obtain better terms; any more than there is any selfish good reason why an employer should not resist the organization of labor if he sees that it would diminish his profits. Justice for the workers of Kenya or Java cannot be argued from the business interests of the British or the Dutch; justice for the tin miners of Bolivia cannot be argued from the profit of American industry. The exploited have to argue their case for themselves in terms of their own interests, and win the moral support of the exploiters; or they have to acquire power to assert themselves and force concessions.

The enlightened selfishness of Great Britain and the enlightened selfishness of the United States may conflict, in which case that which would be best for both, such as a Bretton Woods Agreement, would not agree with the selfish best of either. Both would make concessions. The prosperity of all nations does not come about through the enlightened selfishness of any one nation, but through the counterpressures of selfishness tempered by "a sense of fairness" and resolved by a compromise which represents such rough justice as, on this scale, it is possible to achieve.

Starting with any narrow selfishness, you cannot argue for a more inclusive good in terms of that selfishness pursued with a greater shrewdness or implemented by a more advanced technology. You cannot argue the welfare of the family on the ground of individual selfishness, and so through all the enlarging spheres of class, section, nation, and finally mankind. You cannot argue the welfare of future generations, and hence the conservation of the soil, of timber, and of mineral resources, on the ground of the maximum profit to the present generation.[14]

The only remedy for selfishness is unselfishness, and the gospel of enlightened selfishness can at best be only a step in that direction. Just prosperity has to stand on its own base of justice. The effort to achieve the prosperity of all men throughout all time makes no sense except in its own terms. It makes no sense as merely the means to some lesser prosperity. There is a just prosperity, and there is an unjust prosperity, and only insofar as men prefer justice to injustice will their self-interest coincide with the just prosperity; and that will be because it is just and not because it is their self-interest.

Global economy may be taken to mean not merely a globally extended economy, but a *globally organized* economy.

It is self-evident that economy requires its own specific mechanisms, and that these must correspond in function and range to the nature of the economy. If a national economy requires a national money, then an international economy requires an international money, or at least monetary exchange at a ratio which is sufficiently stable to justify long-range expectations. If banks are necessary within a nation, then international banking is necessary when funds or credits have to be transferred; and an international bank is a reasonable device when loans to a bankrupt or rising economy become a matter of concern to all nations. If it is undesirable that there should be a sharp fluctuation of prices—a sharp depreciation of the exchange value of surpluses laboriously acquired, or a sharp appreciation of the exchange value of goods widely needed—it is reasonable to look for remedies abroad as well as at home. International trade and international markets, like domestic trade and domestic markets, need their appropriate mechanisms.

Such mechanisms—for the regulation of commerce, monetary exchange, credits, and investment, or for the prices of staple commodities—have to be internationally agreed on and internationally organized. Whether this or that specific device is workable and efficient is not here in question. They should, like any social instrument, be subject to amendment in the light of experience. The essential step is that all nations should recognize their necessity and adopt their underlying purpose. As in political organization, so here also the great achievement is the common will. The Bretton Woods Agreement testifies to such a common will. There is a growing body of accepted principles which clarify and define that common will. These principles have been reiterated in the statements of public officials, as, for example, in President Roosevelt's definition of "freedom from want . . . which, translated into world terms, means economic understandings which will secure to every nation a healthy peacetime life for its inhabitants—everywhere in the world." [15] The same emphasis on universality appears in Cordell Hull's radio address of May 18, 1941, in which he declared: (1) that "extreme nationalism must not . . . be permitted to express itself in excessive trade restrictions"; (2) that "nondiscrimination in international trade restrictions must be the rule"; (3) that "raw-material supplies must be available to all nations"; (4) that "the supply of commodities must be so handled as to protect fully the interests of the consuming countries and their people"; (5) that "institutions and arrangements of international finance must be so set up that they lend aid to the essential industries and the continuous development of all countries." These principles are implicit in the Atlantic Charter and in the Mutual Aid Agreement between the United States and Great Britain in which the two parties interpreted the Lend-Lease Act as a means of bettering world-wide economic relations.

A recent statement issued by American economists and businessmen proposes an "International Economic Charter" which presents a comprehensive set of principles, embracing the rights of alien traders; the simplification of customs formalities and procedures; the elimination of unfair competition, subsidies, double taxation, and quantitative restrictions on imports and exports; and provisions for commercial arbitration, exchange control, and tariff adjustments.[16]

To interpret, modify, supplement, and apply these principles there is need of a permanent United Nations economic organization. But if there is to be an international economic policy, it must become public policy, "public" meaning not merely the national public but the international public. Global economy is inseparable from global government and global law. It is quite true that here, as in the nation, the public authorities may hamper economy. But the evils which government may do, and the fears and suspicions to which this gives rise, must not be allowed to blind us to the basic moral function of government. Government is the agency, and the sole agency, to which men can look for the determination and, if needs be, the enforcement of right public policy, including economic policy. For some reason that would bear looking into, those who are entirely willing to accept government as the custodian of political justice are loath to put it in charge of economic justice. Law is the sole agency by which public policy, including economic policy, can be regularized and applied. And it is to government and law, and to these alone, that men can look for the correction of the abuses of government and law, and for the amendment of public policy, including economic policy.

The emphasis on economy in the modern world, and the emphasis on the economic aspects of the one world which is and is to come, revive the old misgivings regarding the place of economic values in human life. These misgivings are well-grounded. The sanction of public approval given to the competitive economy, and the preoccupation of the rising middle class with business, have promoted a cult of calculating selfishness. They have promoted a double standard—the one applicable to the businessman in his business, and the other applicable to the same man in his domestic and other personal relations, and in his moral and religious professions.

Wealth brings power and prestige, which tend to obscure the means by which the wealth was acquired, whether by the practice of some useful art or by the manufacture of chewing-gum or fraudulent patent medicines. Charitable institutions may be founded on what was once called "tainted money"; and there seems to be a growing disposition to forget the taint, and to say that "money is money." Happily the sense of smell is still strong enough to create a feeling of disgust when the grave and tragic news of the war is intermingled with the commercial promotion of tooth paste or lipstick.

The emphasis on economy places a disproportionate emphasis on value-in-exchange which bears little or no relation to moral values, or to any of the values which give human life its dignity and intrinsic worth. The free goods, such as the beauty of nature, or friendship, or the love of God, tend to a low place in human esteem. The enjoyment of Shakespeare or Rembrandt, which costs nothing and is worth nothing in the market, tends to rank below the collectors' possessive interest in the rare first edition or original. The pearls without price are displaced by the commodity of the jeweler.

The values which economy confers have little to do with the essence of human happiness, and shrink in the presence of grave emergencies or when, as sooner or later he must, a man has to come to terms with the universe. According to Adam Smith, who was first a moralist, and second an economist:

Power and riches appear then to be, what they are, enormous and operose machines contrived to produce a few trifling conveniences to the body. . . . They are immense fabrics, which it requires the labour of a life to raise, which threaten every moment to overwhelm the person that dwells in them, and which while they stand, though they may save him from some smaller inconveniencies, can protect him from none of the severer inclemencies of the season. They keep off the summer shower, not the winter storms, but leave him always as much, and sometimes more exposed than before, to anxiety, to fear, and to sorrow; to diseases, to danger, and to death.[17]

This attack on the "dismal science" of economy has the ring of truth, but it is not the whole truth, and like all half-truths it consists half of blindness. Human existence and all human interests have their physical conditions; and even a monastery or a church, dedicated to a higher salvation, requires its economy. The commodities which can be bought and sold, and which are the products of labor that has to be paid for in terms of other products, are sometimes called "means"—as when we speak of "a man of means." This is a good name for him.

Now it is a mistake to forget the ends, but it is no less a

mistake to forget the means; and to forget that all ends whatsoever, when pursued by a physical organism in a physical environment, require physical means. If we disparage means because they are not ends, we should also praise them because they are the means to any ends, from lowest to highest. If they are merely useful, they are immensely and indispensably useful.

The decrying of material goods by those who possess them is not above suspicion. It rarely takes the form of giving them up; more commonly it takes the form of discouraging their possession by others. This might express one's fear of *losing them to others,* or of losing the power derived from their exclusive possession; or it might express one's innocent unawareness of the extent to which these despised material goods condition the goods which one admires. It is not wholly accidental that the economic system as it exists today is submitted to by the poor and enthusiastically applauded by the rich. Those who have prospered most under the system enjoy all the advantages of a strong defensive position; those who have prospered least have to assault a fixed and almost impregnable fortification, and suffer not only from this strategic disadvantage, but from the odium which attaches to troublemakers.

The have-nots of this world are not necessarily inspired by avarice or materialism. They are keenly aware of what they lose by their having-not. They know that it is not possible to enjoy Shakespeare or Rembrandt without an education; or to enjoy nature and friends without leisure; or to engage in any of the "higher things of life" unless they are possessed of the lower things, which are not less indispensable for being lower. Civilization means little to a man living on a subsistence income. In any case, austerity and simplicity should begin at the top and not at the bottom of the economic scale; the gospel of poverty should be taught first to those who have never tried it.

Economic progress in which the benefits of modernized economy shall be justly enjoyed by all, and by which an improved standard of living shall make possible an improved standard of better living, is the economic part of that end which idealists proclaim and which realists labor to achieve. These two moral parties—the idealists and the realists—are here, as elsewhere, inseparable. That is to say, they ought not to be separated. Unhappily, they can be separated. The idealists can merely proclaim and the realists merely labor, the one excessively preoccupied with the goal, the other with the means, the steps, and the difficulties.

The goal is to satisfy men's needs abundantly and justly, the needs of all men everywhere, by the combined efforts and resources of all men everywhere. The fundamental reason, oddly enough, for sending milk to the Hottentots is that the Hottentots want milk. If they do, then getting milk for the Hottentots becomes the duty of everybody that has the milk. If the needy Hottentot were present in the flesh, the man with the milk would give it to him, or at least some of it; and that would be the end, as well as the beginning, of the matter. But in a modern economy, the needy Hottentot tends to be forgotten altogether, and anybody who puts the matter in these simple terms is regarded as a "red," or a Christian, or some other variety of dangerous agitator, like Henry Wallace. And yet the economic system, of whatever proportions and whatever its complications, has no other excuse for being than to get milk to Hottentots. And everybody has an interest in reviving and proclaiming this homely truth; for everybody is somebody's Hottentot.

The solution does not lie, however, in dispatching a bottle of milk from New Hampshire to South Africa. There wouldn't be enough to go round, and it would spoil on the way or soon be used up. If there is to be milk enough for all, including the Hottentots, there must be a dairy industry employing advanced scientific methods. A dairy requires the labor of the dairymen and credit at the bank. If Hottentots are to obtain the milk, it must be condensed and transported, which requires more labor and more capital. All these instrumentalities, and a hundred others in all their vast and intricate ramifications, have to be paid for; which means that all through the system there are men who are staking their livelihood on the parts they play in its operation. Their need of payment is no less imperative than the Hottentots' need for milk. Some people need milk; others need what they can get for milk or for its transportation. It wouldn't help the Hottentot to get milk if the benevolent impulse to help him were to wreck the dairy industry, in New Hampshire or elsewhere, or the transportation system between New Hampshire and Africa.

Furthermore, there are people nearer by who want milk; and it wouldn't help the total lactic situation if the New Englanders went without milk because of the milk sent to the Hottentots. There is much to be said for beginning with the needs at home, and working out from there.

If some global city manager, having no interest of his own at stake except the salary paid him to be disinterested, were to be consulted as to what Americans should do about the Hottentots' need of milk, he would probably advise sending the Hottentots cows so that they could produce their own milk; and to compensate those in America who live on or off their cows, he would suggest that Americans help, or help others to help, the Hottentots to develop products of their own which they could exchange for cows. This would be very different from ignoring the Hottentots. It would idealistically count them in; but at the same time it would realistically reckon with the difficulties that divide the wish from the deed, and the claims of all the parties to the far-flung enterprise by which alone the deed can be accomplished.

Realism in the field of world economy stands for two things: the vested interest which it would be both self-defeating and unjust to deny; and the local interest of self, of family, of neighborhood, of region, and of nation, which define the best place to begin and which form a proper part of the end result.

These realistic considerations of vested interest and proximity are the ballast of an otherwise too flighty idealism. There is another sort of ballast which if allowed to become too heavy prevents movement altogether. This is the ballast of inertia. A contemporary has remarked how many economic slogans between the two wars began with the prefix *re:*

We were successively concerned with reconstruction, retrenchment, reparations, repayment of war debts, revaluation of currencies, restoration of the gold standard, recovery and removal of trade barriers. Even inflation could be made respectable by calling it "reflation." In the 'thirties a leading British expert on international economic relations wrote two books of which the first was called *Recovery* and the second *Security: Can We Retrieve It?* [18]

It is a function of idealism to combat this "nostalgia for the past," or timid acquiescence in the present—this tend-

ency to *re*peat the past, and to *re*main where we are. We
need our Henry Kaisers and our Beardsley Rumls, even
our Henry Wallaces, to remind us of the possibilities as yet
untried. Everything done, even well done, can be done better; even the vast project of human welfare can, for all we
know to the contrary, be compassed by the inventiveness
and consolidated effort of mankind under the leadership
of those who refuse to stand still or to be discouraged.

CHAPTER SIX

World Culture and National Culture

THE term "culture" serves, in the first place, to accent the general fact that the form of human life is made and remade by man himself. "Culture" is opposed to "nature" in order to remind us that men, unlike other animals, are not born already organized, but are equipped with certain faculties, such as reason, conscience, imagination, fellow feeling, and imitativeness, wherewith to organize themselves. Human life is art rather than instinct; changing and creative rather than static; tentative, self-correcting, and progressive rather than finished. It is because of this general and central fact that man can rise so high and sink so low. This is why the term "human" can signify the admirable and godlike, worthy of honor and worship, and also the brutish or less than brutish, deserving of the self-contempt of man himself and punishment at the hands of a just God.

Taken in the antithesis to nature, then, culture is the sum of the arts of life, and of the products of these arts, preserved in records, monuments, and oral tradition, accumulating from age to age, gathered from the past, used and modified in the present, and transmitted to posterity.

Culture also signifies concreteness—the flesh and blood, as distinguished from the bare bones, of life. It embraces the particular ways in which particular social groups have solved their particular problems. Both the interests and the circumstances of life vary from time to time, and from place to place. Every human situation has its uniqueness as well as its generality. Morals, politics, law, economics, education, and religion arise always and everywhere in response to certain constants in life. But the forms which these institutions take will vary infinitely with the materials in which they are embodied. The moral organization of society leaves spheres for the variable exercise of freedom.

There are identical human reflexes, but even no two reflex acts are the same. A sneeze is a sneeze, and yet no two men sneeze alike and no man sneezes twice the same way.[1] Clothes cut after the same model will differ after they are worn; homes built from the same blueprint will differ when they are lived in and become homes. No two acts of justice will be the same—no two political procedures, no two litigations, no two bargains.

Works of sculpture will vary according as they are wrought in granite, marble, clay, or bronze; and likewise the modes of human organization will vary with the flesh and blood in which they are executed. But the materials in which the sculptor works are, as we say, "raw material," having as yet no artistic form; whereas the materials of which human institutions are constructed are already preformed. No man or group of men can be described as *raw* material. A political organization can be carried into effect only by adaptation to beings already having a moral, legal, and economic shape. And the same is true of every other mode of organization, all around the circle. The concrete human life is a locus of interaction in which each institutional practice is modified both by other institutional practices and by a thousand idiosyncrasies of race, temperament, and habitat.

Thus the term "culture" is both a standing protest against abstraction and a recognition of the unique physiognomy of each social life. Human faces are composed of the same features arranged in the same order. But both features and arrangement are capable of infinitely many differences, giving to every face and each of its innumerable expressions a recognizable identity. The idea of culture serves to emphasize this variable wholeness, in which each part reflects every other part, and in which their togetherness yields a peculiar total effect. Culture so conceived is itself an abstraction—albeit the least abstract of abstractions. It invites attention to the shared peculiarities of the group as distinguished from the even more concrete peculiarities of its individual members or subgroups.

It is into such a social concreteness that the individual is born. No child learns to talk in the abstract; he learns to talk his mother tongue and local idiom. So of every element in life. When the new individual learns to do anything, he learns it in the way characteristic of his milieu. The bath in which he is dipped has its peculiar stain, which is at once a camouflage by which he escapes too marked attention and an evidence of normality attested by the approval of his fellows.

When the term "culture" is used by anthropologists, sociologists, and historians, it signifies this social concreteness. There is another use which may seem at first glance to be quite unrelated. The difference is reducible, however, to that between the totality of culture and a selected part. Culture in the broader sense is a characteristic fusion of all the arts by which any given society translates general possibilities into concrete actualities. When the term is so employed, every society has its culture, and all societies have it equally—primitive or barbarous culture is as truly culture as those cultural forms which we distinguish by the name of civilization. Culture in the narrower or selective sense, on the other hand, evaluates cultures and calls certain cultures higher or more advanced.

There are two standards which are commonly employed to evaluate culture. The first is the technological standard. Man is distinguished by the fact that he uses tools. A tool is defined by its use, and it may serve that use more or less well. An advanced culture is then a culture whose tools are relatively improved, thanks to the inventions of science. The second standard is the "humane." This standard requires explanation.

All culture bears the imprint of human nature and exists because it meets some human demand. But it is customary and proper to distinguish two parts of human nature, the appetites and necessities which man shares with all of animal life and the aspirations which are peculiarly his own. We may, therefore, distinguish that part of culture which represents man's basic organic needs for food, shelter, and safety; and that part which represents his so-called higher faculties of reason, imagination, and taste. This part of culture is not more human, but it is more *eminently* human, that is, humane. Roads, bridges, clothing, husbandry, and machines are techniques with which man serves his animal needs and serves them artfully. Poems, paintings, statues, scientific systems, and philosophies are achievements by which man has expressed and satisfied his distinctively human love of beauty, intellectual curiosity, and search for goodness—in short, those passions for perfection which in their sum constitute his spiritual nature.

When we speak of "pure" as distinguished from applied science, and "fine" art as distinguished from useful art, we mean to say that the former contain comparatively less compromise of the humane with the merely human. They express human faculty more directly and freely, without ulterior motive—truth for truth's sake, beauty for beauty's sake, goodness for its own sake. Their objects are not used but enjoyed. They are ideal in a double sense: as images of perfection, and as being valued for their essence rather than for their existence and causal consequences.

The distinction between the technological and humane culture must not be carried to the extreme of supposing that they must be separately embodied. There is a grave danger in such abstraction. They *may* be separated, as when art, morality, science, and religion serve no other purpose than that of creation or contemplation. But humane culture may, and in the highest civilization will, serve to organize, illuminate, and embellish the uses of life.

The advances of the arts of technology which have made the world one in terms of contact and causal interdependence have made for a global unity of culture. Distance and ignorance can no longer be relied on to preserve the oddities of individuals and groups. When plastic objects of different shapes are shaken together in a bag they tend to assume a common form; their angularities and rough edges are smoothed away, and they become as like as two peas; and the same happens with men and societies when they are rubbed together.

The most evident tendency to cultural sameness is in the technological arts, where the latest improvements and gadgets rapidly spread to all parts of the world. The force of imitation passes them from group to group; the force of prestige passes then from more advanced to more backward groups; and no group can now escape the effects of these forces. When such conformities are superficial and partial, they produce strange incongruities, like the naked savage in the missionary's top hat; but the rest of the wardrobe soon follows the hat, and European clothes tend to sweep the field.

European clothes may not be adopted for their greater usefulness, still less for their greater beauty. But the deeper uniformities of technology are due to the fact that there are more or less efficient ways of doing the same things, and that the more efficient tends to supersede the less, not only in the vertical line of temporal progress, but in the lateral lines of spacial spread.

The increased range of human intercourse tends to global unity also in the realm of humane culture. Indigenous literatures are widely disseminated, translated, and sometimes even read. Art forms are borrowed, exchanged, repeated, and commingled. Monuments of art are visited by tourists, or imported from abroad. In whatever country they are situated, museums collect and exhibit the art of all countries. All nations tend to share their past as well as their present. All human treasures, however created, acquired, and accumulated, tend to become parts of one terrestrial store shared and enjoyed by all men.

There is, then, a trend to global culture. There is a trend to a common standard of living, on the level of convenience and utility; and a trend to the interchange and common possession of the fruits of genius and the higher arts. These uniformities, combined with the all-pervasive effects of imitation and prestige, will undoubtedly tend, in increasing degrees, to produce a terrestrial and all-human physiognomy which would be remarked by a visitor from Mars. As men live together they tend to live alike; and as *all* men live together they will *all* tend to live alike.

This concrete terrestrial uniformity will provide the necessary social basis for world institutions, analogous to that which the cultures of local groups and nations provide for their narrower institutions. But what will be the effect upon culture itself, and in particular upon humane culture? How can culture be fitted to the requirements of international peace and co-operation without loss of those specific values which it contributes to human life? There are two issues at stake, both of which must be submitted to the same ultimate moral standard: the issue of freedom versus control, and the issue of individuality versus universality. Does global unity tend through excessive control to rob culture of its essential freedom? Does global unity tend through excessive emphasis on the universal to rob culture of its essential individuality? The two questions are not sharply separable, but they provide a convenient order of topics.

Why should culture be free? First, because men and groups like and desire their own cultures; and not because diverse cultures afford a pageant for Cook's parties who enjoy the quaint customs of the natives. Because, in the second place, the area of culture is the area *left free,* and *made free,* by conscience, politics, law, and economy. It is the role of these institutions to prescribe, in broad terms, what men may and may not do; and it is the role of culture to exercise choice within these limits. It is the role of institutions to create as much freedom as possible; it is the role of culture to use it as fully as possible. This, at any rate, is the relation of free institutions to freedom. The purpose of totalitarian institutions is to leave as little freedom as possible; or to leave freedom only to the whole, and to the parts only vicariously or as acting in its name. It is to be assumed at this stage of the argument that world institutions are to be based on the liberal and not on the totalitarian model; and that they will be more rather than less liberal than national institutions, since they can entrust the greater part of social control to the latter. If national institutions do not find it necessary to interfere with cultural freedom, still less should international institutions.

In the third place, culture should be free because culture is the source of all freedom, and if freedom be denied to culture, freedom is killed at the source. Technological culture gives men the tools with which their freedom is implemented, or with which they can *do* what they choose; humane culture presents the options of choice, and stimulates the faculties of reason, taste, and imagination which are the faculties of choice. Without freedom of culture even the institutions which limit freedom cannot be freely chosen, or made effective.

As the friend of cultural freedom the global order will have to deal with the enemies of cultural freedom, of which there are two which call for special comment: nationalism and imperialism. The modern state, imbued with nationalistic frenzy, may deprive its minorities of their cultural freedom by the exercise of political and legal controls; and the minority in order to preserve its cultural freedom may seek to establish its own independent political and legal controls.

The Soviet idea of diverse nationalities within a single political jurisdiction—an idea peculiarly dear to Marshal

Stalin, who is a Russian in politics and a Georgian in nationality—presents an interesting solution of this problem. It is true that the solution is complicated by the fact that in Soviet Russia there must be not only political but economic conformity—one union and one socialism, represented by the dictatorship of the Communist party. But the system, even under these limitations, is fruitful of cultural freedom. It represents a serious attempt to appease the sentiment of nationality, and to enlist its support, by limiting its area. Ukrainians, for example, are to be permitted, encouraged, and helped to be as nationalistically Ukrainian as they like in their ethnic solidarity, their language and folklore, their literature and art, and now presumably even in their religion, provided they conform with the other Soviet nationalities to the same united polity and the same form of economy. Here, then, is an experience and a precedent available to whatever form of international control may in the future be created. National cultures can sometimes be conserved, and national aspirations satisfied, without altering existing political structures. Cultural, political, or even economic units do not necessarily coincide, and the nationalistic sentiment may be identified with any one of them as may best suit the existing situation. And perhaps it is true to say that the sentiment of nationality is in the long run most deeply identified with cultural elements which are separable from politics and economy.[2]

The identification of cultural, political, and economic divisions has led to the modern form of imperialism, in which the strong assume political control over the weak in order to trade with them, and show little or no respect for their cultures. These empires—British, Dutch, French, American—all feel the prevailing wind, and are now pre-

pared to concede cultural self-determination in order to
relieve the pressure for political independence, or as a step
in that direction. A former Governor of the French African colony of Tchad has recently described what he terms
"The New Colonial Policy of France." After laying down
the general maxim that the imperial power acts as a
trustee in the interest of the dependent society, he goes on
to state the doctrine that such groups can become civilized
and self-governing only in terms of their own cultural traditions. He writes:

The old French colonial policy revolved about the conception of more and less *advanced* civilizations. The new policy
revolves about the idea of *different* civilizations. . . . Even in
the "darkest" and most primitive parts of Africa, France has
never found a political vacuum; everywhere are ancestral habits,
political customs, a judicial or religious code—all the elements of
civilization. . . . The basic approach for us Frenchmen . . . is
a desire to recognize those traits in the natives that are common to all men. But the foundation on which this policy rests
must be an understanding of the relation between such universality and the nature of things distinctively African.[3]

International polity, whether on grounds of justice or
on grounds of expediency, must respect and protect the
rights of social groups to possess their own cultures, and to
advance from backwardness or enjoy modernness in their
own several ways. Thus cultural decentralization, in turn,
serves the cause of unity. Free cultures become partners
and mutual benefactors. Each, having something to give,
contributes its own gifts. Devotees of the same cult form
bonds of sympathy and understanding regardless of other
bonds that may divide them. Private relations may prevail over public differences. Stefan Zweig said, speaking
of his literary friends, "One was in Germany, another in

France, another in Italy, and yet they were all in the same homeland, for they lived in poetry alone." [4] No one can live by poetry alone, or by science, or by any cultural vocation, but these vocations do create common homelands which ignore the barriers which divide politically organized societies. The recognition of another as a fellow scientist or artist is sometimes the first step toward recognizing him as a man.

Humane culture is the product of an individual person and not of a society. Hence the freedom which humane culture requires and exercises is the freedom which the society extends to its members. Here the role of global unity is to permit and help its component societies not merely to develop and preserve their several social cultures, but to make those cultures free, to the end that the total life of man may be a free association of free cultures.

The essential freedom of science is the freedom of the scientist. It is his freedom from every other control in order that he may submit his mind to the evidence. When there actually is evidence, the scientist is bound by it and as a scientist he can acknowledge no prior allegiance. If the facts verify his hypothesis, he must accept it; if the facts disprove the hypothesis, he must reject it. He must draw from premises the conclusion which they imply. If he is to be thus faithful to the evidence, he must be neither bribed nor intimidated; he must be governed by no passion but the love of truth; he must be delivered from the insidious influences of prejudice, habit, imitation, and public favor.

This is the freedom of the scientist at the moment of his responsible scientific affirmation; in this freedom he must be schooled by training and self-discipline, and protected and assisted by society. For if society is to enjoy the fruits of true knowledge, society must respect and cherish those acts of mind by which true knowledge is created. Science, like all other forms of organized activity, must have a place in public policy and be supported by those who, though they cannot make science, can appreciate its requirements and provide for them. The support of science is a duty of citizenship in each political society and in the world at large.

But scientific freedom, like any freedom, becomes a right only when it is limited within a system of rights. Science, both as an achievement and as a pursuit, is a part of life and has to submit to the larger requirements imposed by the whole of life. This does not mean that any other influence should intervene between the evidence and the conclusion, or that the scientific mind should be corrupted. But granting that science is not science at all unless it is free within itself, there still remains the question of the place of this freedom among other freedoms. To say that only free science can be true is not the same as to say that true science or its pursuit is always good. In order to deal with this question it is necessary to apply to science as science those moral principles which underlie the major human institutions of politics, law, and economy.

Science is to be credited with its disinterestedness, and tends, therefore, to promote that attitude of mind which is the essence of moral judgment. Being itself free from any interest save its own proper interest in truth, science judges all other interests, when it judges them at all, impartially or objectively; it is free from the subjective bias which causes the mind to ignore interests, or to weigh them lightly, when they fall outside some narrow circle of warmth and intimacy. To the scientific mind, as to the "judicial" mind, an interest is an interest, no matter whose it be. The spirit of pure science is a counterforce to selfishness.

The scientific interest is essentially nonacquisitive. It does not need exclusive possession of its object, and can consume without destroying it. Two minds can perceive or think the same object without conflict. The scientific interest fits intrinsically, without alteration, into that harmony of interests which morality seeks to achieve.

Pure science is humane; that is, it expresses the distinctive human capacity of reason and satisfies man's "higher" nature. At the same time it is infinitely useful. The causal knowledge and power of prediction which it yields serve the interests which morality harmonizes, and the institutions—political, legal, and economic—by which this harmony is carried into effect. Science is an indispensable condition of all achievement, including moral achievement.

So much for the credit side of the account. On the other hand, all science save moral science is in itself morally indeterminate. It judges what is and not what ought to be. Science and its applications serve God or Mammon, peace or war, the Axis or the Allies, with equal willingness. As has been recently remarked, the chemist, qua chemist, does not "ask whether his formula will kill a house rat or a housewife." [5]

The moral character of the infinite usefulness of science depends on the uses to which it is put. These uses have to be morally controlled, by conscience and by public policy. Because the biological sciences are used for healing purposes by the physician, and the physical sciences for the purposes of a constructive civilization, we forget that these benefits depend not only on biology and physics themselves but on the social codes of medicine and engineering.

The pursuit of science depends on the leisure created by an economy; its freedom is a privilege protected by free institutions. The scientist who ignores this is a moral escapist or at best an innocent whom it may pay society to maintain as a public charge. A persuasive and good-tempered presentation of this escapist doctrine is to be found in Albert J. Nock's recent autobiography, *Memories of a Superfluous Man.* Endorsing Voltaire's famous *"Il faut cultiver notre jardin,"* he adds:

> The only thing that the psychically-human being can do to improve society is to present society with *one improved unit.* ... I learned early with Thoreau that a man is rich in proportion to the number of things he can afford to let alone; and in view of this I have always considered myself extremely well-to-do. All I ever asked of life was the freedom to think and say exactly what I pleased, when I pleased, and as I pleased.[6]

Is that all! What a modest demand! All he asks is a reign of law; an order of freedom, tolerance, and security; an opportunity for education; and a social system in which the world's work is so well done as to permit spheres of superfluity such as the author himself so graciously occupies. This is essentially the doctrine of the social parasite, who would eat his cake and let others bake it. It represents an unsportsmanlike willingness to profit without contributing—to be carried in the boat without pulling one's weight.

It will be a function of the postwar world to proclaim the dependence of science on freedom, and to protect and equip that freedom; at the same time it will be a duty of that world to see to it that science is not only useful, but used for good ends. There is a reciprocal duty of scientists to play their part as citizens in supporting the institutions, general and specific, national and international, on which their privileges depend, and in championing the moral purpose by which these privileges are justified.

The fine arts, like science, make their own peculiar contribution to human good, and if they are to make this contribution, they must be free to do so. The artist who in his artistic activity allows other considerations to overrule the dictates of taste or beauty is like the pure scientist who allows alien influences to divert him from the evidence; he, too, must have his code of purity and rigor. Art, like science, may be pursued for its own sake—science for science's sake, art for art's sake. But here, too, there is the same ulterior appeal to moral principles.

For art, like science, is a part of life, both in the pursuit and in the achievement. The intrinsic motive of the fine arts is the joy of artistic creation and the aesthetic appreciation of its works. There must be a freedom to enjoy these joys and a freedom to perfect their objects in their own terms. But these freedoms, like all freedoms, must be balanced against other freedoms, and find their proper place in a system of freedoms.

Art is useful—not only the technological arts whose essence is utility, but the fine arts, which in their essence are ends in themselves. If they are the mere servants of propaganda, they are unfaithful, and will fail to yield their own peculiar fruit; but being free, they can the more effectively serve any cause to which they lend themselves. Through creating symbols they augment the appeal of love, or gain, or ambition, or war, or patriotism. They can strengthen the appeal of truth, through representing truly; the appeal of virtue, through representing its triumph; and the appeal of the moral end, through creating images of perfection.

The fine arts, like science, are essentially nonacquisitive. Artistic creation and aesthetic appreciation need not deprive others of their objects; they do not divide men against one another, but tend rather to unite them in associated enjoyment of a common object.

But literature, painting, sculpture, and music are, like science, in themselves morally neutral. This gives them the same quality of disinterestedness, but the same promiscuity. It is true that art has its own inner logic, but the theme is infinite. It may represent the triumph of evil over good, as the most tragic of all tragedies. It may in representing one aspect of reality misrepresent its other aspects. It may excite evil passions or good. There is Plato's Ionian and Lydian music of "softness and indolence," and his Dorian and Phrygian music of "necessity and freedom."[7]

The aesthetic attitude is morally irresponsible. Aesthetic enjoyment justifies the parts by the whole, whereas morality justifies the whole by the parts. Morality organizes the whole of life so as to preserve and enhance its constituent interests and persons, but aesthetic enjoyment accepts any parts which compose an organic whole. Morality finds value in a tragic opposition of parts by seeing its tragic wholeness; morality reorganizes it in order to remove the tragedy. Aesthetic enjoyment makes men spectators of the struggle between good and evil rather than partisans of good. In so doing it weakens the moral will.

There is little, if any, correlation between aesthetic and moral sensibility. The degree to which the artist can dissociate his vocation from virtue and duty finds proof in the shocking story of the "gentle flute player" who became a Gestapo agent and was recently shot by Norwegian patriots for his unparalleled brutality:

It was in the early thirties, when economic depression gripped most of the world, that a German musician arrived in the Norwegian capital, summoned by the Oslo Symphony Orchestra. . . . What a flute player he was! He excelled in Haydn, in Mozart, but whatever he played, his listeners were ecstatic. Fellow musicians, artists, the critics, intellectuals of every field became his devotees and friends. . . . Solemn, tender, sad-eyed, retiring, he seemed fashioned of too fragile stuff to cope with a world of discord. . . . Vividly I recall his tenderness, how this gentleman lived in and talked of his dream world of Mozart and song. Here was the true German artist.

On the evening of April 8, 1940, in the privacy of his home, the melancholy artist shed his mask. The sad eyes melted into two glowing pools of hate. . . . Orders had come through from Berlin. From a remote recess of his wardrobe he produced . . . his Gestapo uniform. Through that night he worked over his files and dossiers on Norway and Norwegians, records of the innocent conversations of his Oslo benefactors, his friends, his acquaintances. . . . The flutist, Rolf Schüttauf, left his apartment for a rendezvous with his chief—Heinrich Himmler! [8]

Like the scientist, the artist is tempted by his vocation to ignore the moral foundations on which it rests. Stefan Zweig has written of a literary circle which he knew in Paris before the First World War:

These were poets who make no demands on society—neither the regard of the masses nor decorations, honors or profit—who sought only to bind verse to verse in silent yet passionate effort, every line saturated with music, flaming with color, glowing with images. They constituted a guild, an almost monastic order in the midst of our clattering time; to them, awaredly rejecting life's workaday round, nothing in the whole universe was more significant than the note—delicate, yet surviving the booming of the age—emitted when rhyme joining rhyme created the indescribable stir, softer than the sound of a leaf falling in the wind, that vibrates to the most distant soul.[9]

Stefan Zweig was mistaken in saying that these painters or musicians who enjoyed the freedom of Paris made no demands on society. They demanded that freedom, and their demand was satisfied. And behind that freedom stood the institutions which created the freedom. One, at least, of those men—Charles Péguy—volunteered at the outset of the First World War, saying that he considered it "ill-bred to ask for victory and not to feel like fighting." [10]

He who profits from freedom and requires its victory, but at the same time avoids the battle, is only a fraction of a man, however great an artist. It is this which accounts for the odium which attaches to the "aesthete" and his "ivory tower." This goes for every sort of battle, whether physical or moral. It applies to the writer who says that "if you are called to the intellectual life, then you had better remain single and, if possible, celibate." [11] Epochs of cosmopolitanism when, as in the Hellenistic Age, men meet and mingle in some metropolis on the common ground of higher culture, have a taint of decadence because of political duties neglected and escaped.

Society can, and should, afford the artist's irresponsibility; society will profit by its fruits. But the artist should accept his privileges with humility and a tinge of self-reproach. For his irresponsibility has to be compensated elsewhere. Someone must secure the foundations and protect the walls of his ivory tower, and provide its occupant with the necessities of life.

A global society will nourish, implement, and safeguard

the freedom of artistic genius among all the races of men. Clive Bell has said that "the one good thing Society can do for the artist is to leave him alone." This is a permissible counterblast to censoriousness and the harnessing of art to alien uses. But society cannot, strictly speaking, leave anybody alone; being left alone is itself a privilege bestowed on man by organized society, as this writer himself affirms when he goes on to say that Society can do something for art, because it can increase liberty . . . protect minorities . . . and defend originality from the hatred of the mediocre mob." [12] By its institutions, both national and international, society must reconcile artistic freedom with the requirements of justice and humanity, and it may fairly ask that art out of its freedom shall provide symbols wherewith to strengthen their appeal.

The development of a global culture raises not only the question of control but the question of universality. Here also there is a possible loss to be reckoned with—the loss of those characteristics of culture which express the local, the indigenous, the intimate, the personal, the ethnic, and the national. The two issues are interrelated, and often confounded; for universality is sometimes attained by denying the freedom to differ. But they are essentially different. The question now raised is whether the value of culture is heightened or diminished by universality, however it be attained, whether by force or by the unforced effects of inertia, habit, imitation, learning, imagination, or thought.

Anthropologists, having first emphasized the multiplicity of cultures, now recognize the uniformity which arises from the fact that different societies, having the similar basic "drives" and external stimuli, learn similar lessons by trial and error, and acquire similar habits. Thus a recent writer enumerates seventy-five items which occur in all known human societies—items such as fire-making, funeral rites, government, family, property, tools, and language. Each of these items is capable of further specification, but they reveal a universal culture pattern.[13] In proportion as the world is causally unified, this uniformity of independent cultures, in which men learn the same thing from the same conditions, will be increasingly supplemented by intercultural uniformity in which men learn from one another.

There can be no doubt of the tendency to universality in the practical arts. There is a "know-how" which, wherever it originates, is soon adopted elsewhere, and spreads more rapidly and widely through the greater closeness of contact and the ease of intercourse which now is obtained between man and man over the whole surface of the earth.

This does not pass without protest. Those who are accustomed to the old way dislike the new, and those who are accustomed to the local way dislike the way imported from abroad. A Kanaka chief in Micronesia is represented as saying:

We do not need clothing—the sunshine clothes us. We do not need an iron roof to carry rain water into a cement tank. The water that streams down the trunk of a tree can be turned into a jar. We do not need farming tools of iron and steel. We can make our own from the shell of the giant clam. We do not need alarm clocks and phonographs and electric lights. They spoil the sounds of the forest and the light of the moon. We do not need the telephone—we can talk to those on faraway plantations through the shell-trumpet. We do not need schools. The father can teach his children all that is necessary for our simple manner of life. We do not need hospitals. This is a small island—if some did not die there would soon be too many people, too little food. But our young men are upset by the idea that they must do something, even if it is something useless. On the athletic field near the school a track has been made where boys may run around in a circle. That is what civilization is—running around in a circle.[14]

If this complaint is authentic and typical, then the United States might do well to import wit and wisdom from Micronesia—but not in place of houses and hospitals. The trend to uniformity in the applied arts is not due primarily to blindness, but to intelligence. If people want to dispose of waste, or communicate with one another, or preserve their food, or prolong their lives, or protect themselves from cold, it is intelligent of them to acquire a sewage system, a telephone service, refrigeration, hospitals, and houses—all of the latest model, because here the latest is usually proved by experience to be the best. If a society needs clothes and employment, and if its members can raise cotton, it is intelligent of them to put these things together and organize an economy. Even Gandhi, despite his odd paucity of clothes, is said to be in favor of the development in India of a textile industry which will, no doubt, resemble those of Manchester or Fall River.

An advanced society, in the technological sense, is a society well-equipped to do what it wants to do. There may be something wrong with what a well-equipped society does with its equipment; but, given what it does, there is nothing wrong with its equipment. That is the fundamental reason why those who want to do similar things borrow its equipment.

All this means merely that when people learn of a quicker, more adequate, and less wasteful way of accomplishing what they are trying to accomplish, they will adopt that way if they can. They can be prevented from doing so only by denying them the knowledge and the power. On what ground such restrictive measures could be justified is difficult to say. It is certainly not to be expected that backward societies should remain backward in order to be picturesque, and thus afford entertainment to spectators who live in advanced hotels.

Since technical knowledge is now widely disseminated, and since its products are easily and profitably transported, we may as well make up our minds that in the long run men will use the same tools—from minor gadgets to large-scale industries. The things which are most useful will be generally used, and the machinery of life will be similar over the whole earth. This process is both irreversible in fact, and morally desirable. There will still remain abundant room for diversity in what people make with their tools, in the refinement of their tools, in the ends which they seek, in their personal experiences and relations—in all those parts of life which are not tools, and which the possession of improved tools makes more abundant. In fact, the primitive uniformities are more monotonous and more rigid than the advanced. It is quite possible for people to develop originality and difference despite the uniformity of their modern plumbing; and when they fail to do so, it is not the fault of the plumbing.

On the humane level of culture the problem of universality assumes a different form. The products of science and the fine arts tend, like any other human products, to be widely disseminated in a physically unified world. But the deeper question here is of another order—not a question of distribution, but a question of validity. Are truth and beauty universally valid, or are they valid only relatively to some particular unit of human life? Is there something in the meaning of science and of art which implies or which prohibits their universality? Would universality fulfill, or would it destroy, their purpose?

This question of validity has to be distinguished not only from the question of distribution but from the question of origin. Both science and the fine arts originate somewhere and express the genius of some particular person and group. This fact might be thought to contradict their universality. They may be valid for all men by virtue of appealing to the man in men, or because of inviting the attention of all men to the same objects; but they must also reflect the peculiar social conditions under which they arise. Professor Werner Jaeger, in a book which has contributed greatly to our understanding of this subject, emphasizes the universality of humane culture and at the same time argues that it is characteristically Greek. Speaking of the Sophists he writes:

They held that the ideal of culture was the climax of civilization in the broadest and most universal sense, which embraces everything between the first rude attempts of man to impose his will on elemental nature, and the highest self-education and self-shaping of the human spirit. . . . [They] revealed once more the true nature of the Greek spirit, its concentration on the universal, the *whole* of life.[15]

The contradiction is, however, only apparent. An object does not necessarily possess the particularity of the subject which has dealings with it. Fish are not Norwegian because Norwegians fish them out of the sea; a wide view may be had from a narrow eminence. There may be a particular aptitude for universality. A human mind nourished by the soil in which its roots are laid may nonetheless bear fruit relished by men of other times and places. A society may be so constituted as to deliver its own members from bondage. The creative or critical spirit which soars above its origins may nevertheless be a product of these origins. It may be characteristic of Greek antiquity, or of France in the twelfth century, or of Italy in the fifteenth century, or of England in the eighteenth century, that it should be more than Greek, Italian, French, or English. Likewise Europe as a whole, and because of its continental characteristics, is the mother of what is called European civilization; and even though Europe should, like ancient Greece, lose its political leadership, its cultural gifts may yet be valid for all mankind and all posterity.

Is cultural relativism, which is in some sense an indisputable fact, prejudicial to science and the fine arts—a defect to be minimized—or is it a merit to be consciously exploited? The answer is not the same for science and the fine arts, and they must therefore be separately considered.

It has remained for modern Fascism and Nazism to carry the tribal ideal of culture to the extreme length of applying it to the exact sciences. Instead of confessing to relativism as a more or less unavoidable human limitation, they have boldly adopted it as a standard. Thus spoke Mussolini:

> If relativism signifies the end of faith in science, the decay of that myth, "science," conceived as the discovery of absolute truth, I can boast of having applied relativism to the analysis of socialism. If relativism signifies contempt for fixed categories and men who claim to be the bearers of an external objective truth . . . then there is nothing more relativistic than Fascist attitudes and activity. . . . It is sufficient to have a single fixed point: the nation.[16]

If the nation is the fixed point, and there are several nations, then there are several fixed points. This, of course, is the trouble with scientific relativism. Nazism took another fixed point, and held that there was a Germanic mathematics and physics, and a non-Germanic mathematics and physics, and that the former were better because they were Germanic. This was a heroic affirmation, clearly contradicted by the history and meaning of science. If the Germans have a wrong idea they are likely to make the worst of it—this, at least, is characteristically German. But it is harder to fly in the face of the facts even than to fly in the face of an enemy air force; and here the Nazi creed of self-assertion did not succeed even at home. For the science which the Nazis used, not for academic preferment but as the basis for technology, was a universal science, shared with their non-Germanic enemies.

Even were science characteristically Greek or German in its origin, it would still be nonnational and nonethnic in its intent and in its perfected form. Professor Jaeger recognizes this distinction:

Euclidean geometry and Aristotelian logic are even now permanent sets of principles for the operation of the mind, and cannot possibly be put aside. Yet even these intellectual laws, universally valid, and purged of all temporal content, were created by Greek science; are, when viewed with a historical eye, Greek through and through. . . . And this is still more true of the other works of the Greek mind, which still bear the stamp of the age and nation that made them, and are directly connected with a definite historical situation.[17]

When any work of science takes its place in the corpus of science, it is purged, so far as possible, of "the stamp of the age and nation that made" it, in order that it may be "universally valid." The accident of its origin gives way to the essence of its truth. This holds in varying degrees of all knowledge, including history, philosophy, and the moral sciences.

The reason is to be found in the purpose of science, which is to reflect the nature of things "out there" as they are in themselves, in the world common to all knowing minds. Science is essentially self-denying and not self-expressive. It tries to eliminate the personal equation—the idiom and the idiosyncrasy. This does not mean that it is not active in its art of discovery, and its framing and invention of theories, but that the final test of a theory is its correspondence to the fact, its revelation of being, or its consistency with other theories which themselves satisfy this objective test.

It is also the purpose of science to reflect the *general* nature of things. It is universal not only in its objectivity, but in its objects. Knowledge of particular regions of nature is not yet fully science. Knowledge of the flora and fauna of Alaska or of the stars of the southern skies must be subsumed under the laws of biology and astrophysics. Scientific problems tend to be taken into laboratories, where even the data of observation are identical. Scientists tend to speak a common language, and to employ technical terms and symbols, because for science linguistic differences, with their historical and emotional meanings, are irrelevant. Science thus moves, under the impulse of its own refinement and self-criticism, away from the unique personal and social experiences to the common characteristics of common objects.

Scientists, speaking a common language, and intent upon the same characteristics of the same world, are united in a common task. They build science together, each scientist confirming, and building on, the work of every other scientist—all in full view both of one another and of the building so far built. The cleavages that divide nation from nation, or even past from present, mean nothing to them in terms of their scientific vocation, and in this they set an example and pave the way for other vocations.

Because they co-operate, they organize, and because they co-operate internationally, they organize internationally. They have international congresses and unions, and are laying plans for their future development and permanence. A recent compilation lists some forty such international congresses, unions, commissions, bureaus, and sections, representing physics, engineering, chemistry, geology, medicine, biology, anthropology, and psychology. The following claim is made by an officer of one of these organizations:

If there is any nucleus of international goodwill and understanding left in the world, it resides, I think, in scientific personnel. They will be the first to mend the broken wires of communication, and I hope this time all the world will realize, whether we like it or not, that we have to live together on a globe which science has made too small for war.[18]

It is said that war stimulates scientific progress, not merely because of an intensified demand for the applications of science, but also because of the closer co-operation of scientists working together for the national cause. But the injury which war does to science outweighs its benefits. For war corrupts the purity of science, narrows attention to its military uses, and separates the scientists of each nation from their scientific coworkers in other nations. Hence science has a stake in the achievement of peace.

The universality of science unites men in their scientific pursuit, but this in itself does not overcome the narrowness of that pursuit. Happily, when scientists gather in congresses and unions, they meet not only scientists but also men and citizens interested not only in their several sciences but also in the relation of science to society. It is clear that if all men were scientists, and all scientists were preoccupied with their scientific vocation, there could be no science, for lack of these fundamental moral institutions on which all vocations depend. And the universality of science does not provide for the claims of that concreteness and individuality of which the fine arts are the foremost protagonists.

Poets, painters, sculptors, and musicians do not co-operate, neither do they organize. Nor do they, like the scientist, endeavor to purge the universal of the personal or social angle from which it is approached. Subjectivity, which for science is a taint to be removed, is for the fine arts a part of the essence to be preserved. The fine arts begin and end with an individual experience.

There is, first, that individual experience which constitutes the theme or subject matter. This experience may be an experience *of* the more or less universal, and it may be a more or less universal *experience;* but in either case it retains the character of a perspective. If its object is universal, then it is the universal approached *by* somebody *from* somewhere; however wide the arc which it subtends, its angle narrows to a point of view. And if the experience itself is universal, this means that others can transpose themselves to its point of view, or, because it is so broadly human, find that they already occupy it. To put the matter in the simplest terms, the natural scene composes a landscape, wide or narrow, to an observer stationed at a certain place. Another can see that landscape because he can put himself in the observer's place, on the same mountain-top; or because the place itself is so generalized that as human beings his place and the observer's are the same, as when both view the starry heavens from the surface of the earth.

This is a gross oversimplification. The perspective cannot be defined merely in terms of space and time. The subject brings to it much more than an angle of observation; his point of view embraces the deposit of his previous experience, conscious and unconscious. It is this which gives the experience its unique meaning, both emotional and ideational. But this richness of subjectivity can still be largely shared by another, either vicariously, or by finding a similar subjectivity in himself, as when a man is invited to view his worldly attachments from the standpoint of approaching death.

Such individuated experiences are immediately agreeable. Consciousness dwells on them, holds them in suspense, and gladly remains within their boundaries. They appeal to an inherent bias in human apprehension—what the eyes prefer to see, the ears to hear, and each of the several faculties to feed itself upon. The primary aesthetic object, the theme, or subject matter, is some whole of experience in which these faculties play their several interlocking roles—sense, intellect, emotion, memory, all held together and held at arm's length in their immediate enjoyment. The fine arts owe their all-pervasiveness in human life to the fact that such experiences lie within the range of all men's consciousness at all times. The enjoyment of them is the aesthetic interest. It asks no questions. Science asks, What is the explanation? and passes on to theories. Practice asks, What shall be done about it? and adopts some plan of action. The aesthetic interest prolongs, renews, and savors the experience itself.

This might be the whole of man's aesthetic life, and is the whole for many men: simply to select for immediate enjoyment from among the experiences which the natural and human scene affords. Life abounds in unities of line and color, in stories long and short, and in lyric moods. But the same impulse which prompts men to hold such experiences in their minds prompts them to give them a more lasting physical embodiment by which they may be recovered at will, or communicated to others. Hence the second aesthetic object, which we call the work of art. It embodies the original experience in some sensory medium of words, tones, colors, lines, by which it is captured, and through which it can be recaptured or recognized. This embodiment has in turn to be individually experienced; and now the medium, as well as the original theme, has its own delightfulness of quality, form, and fitness.

Thus several interests work together—the interest in the original theme, the interest in the medium, the interest in creation, and the interest in recognition. Fine art may be judged by any or all of these standards.

The term "contemplation" is sometimes used to indicate that aesthetic enjoyment is not concerned with the existence of its theme. It deals with the imaginary rather than with the real, or treats the real as though it were imaginary. It is concerned with *what* its object is, rather than with the fact *that* it is, or is not. It thus differs from both knowledge and practice. But it contributes to both. To knowledge it contributes the values of immediacy, concreteness, and the fine discrimination of qualities and relationships; to practice it contributes the vivid awareness of ideals. It enables the mind to hold in view what it is the existence of which is in question, or is to be achieved. The fine arts call upon the imagination, and repay it themselves, thus serving all the uses of imagination, theoretical and practical, free of cost.

The fine arts draw their themes from the artist's actual experience, and that experience will reflect his natural and social environment. If the artist is Russian, his experience will be Russian, embracing something of Russian life and physical setting, and something of Russian traditions, habits, and national attitudes. The medium, too, whether verbal or sensory, will be in some degree Russian in quality and in form. The following is a description of Russian music as of 1848—a symphonic treatment by Glinka of two Russian airs, a wedding song and dance song:

The first simple utterance of that Russian theme is not a tune, only, but a landscape and a people. It has no date. The material is all the mediaeval centuries, in the sense in which that miracle could be achieved in a line of poetry, with this difference that Glinka did not write the tune, he discovered it and gave it immortality. In its origin it can have been no better than a hundred other Russian airs, but his genius sharpened and pointed it, so that it is, at once, Russian and individual, of Glinka's own. The dance song that follows it, so Russian and characteristic in its preluding, in the manner in which announcement is made that it is coming, points the alternative season of the year. The first tune is the Russian winter: this is a long summer night, miles from anywhere, lost in the huge distances, among the wooden houses of a remote village, in a haze of dust while the immense sun is setting. Nothing of an outer world has come to them. All has been the same for centuries, since the time that they were pagan.[19]

This music, in other words, is human, medieval, national, and finally personal, in the experience which it reflects. If it were not, it would lack depth and sincerity. These are the standards to be applied to the nationality

of art. The Nazi party once issued the following pro-
nouncement:

> So long as there remains in Germany any unpolitical, neutral,
> liberal or individualistic art, our task is not ended. There must
> no longer be a single artist who creates otherwise than nation-
> ally and with a national purpose. Every artist who withdraws
> from this preoccupation must be hunted as an enemy of the
> nation until he gives up his intolerable resistance.

The Soviet Union once similarly prescribed that its artists
should be "saturated with the heroic struggle of the international proletariat." [20]

The question here is the question not merely of the
artist's freedom, but of the range and genuineness of his
experience. A democrat will rightly express his democratic
experience in art, a Christian his Christianity, a Nazi his
Nazism, and a Communist his Communism. But if he is
subjected to external pressures, the experience which he
expresses will be narrowly limited, and it may not be
authentic. That which is local and personal in art should
be inevitable and spontaneous. It should not be forced,
nor should it be confined at the expense of the universal.
The relation of art to nationality is accidental. The most
advanced music, for example, is Western or European, in
its technique and in its public. Its composers and critics
have learned from one another, regardless of any narrower
geographical or political division; and there is nothing in
the genius of music itself which forbids the extension of its
province to the limits of communication. "Great works of
art" may be, if as yet it can scarcely be said that they are,
"precious products of a common effort not of a tribe, a
group, a nation, but of humanity. As such, they give us
hope, and promise better things to come." [21]

When the themes of art are free and genuine, they will embrace what is universal as well as what is personal and local in experience. All human experience is some human being's version of the all-human experience, or the common lot. It calls into play the same general faculties; feels the same mortal vicissitudes of love, work, and death. And in rendering its themes the fine arts employ, again with local and personal variations, the same media—the same sensory elments, and the same variety of forms. They have a double universality—of the subject and of the object—the universality of human nature and the universality of relationships and meanings which the imagination can divorce from circumstance and communicate to the imagination of others.

In proportion as the life of mankind is unified, there will be a culture of the world in a double sense. There will be a foundation of sameness, and there will be a community of differences. All men will tend to become alike in the techniques and tools with which they satisfy their needs. They will become alike by living together, and if they are to live together in peace and mutual helpfulness, they must acquire a likeness of attitude in respect of their common concerns. Their literature and art will tend to reflect their common experiences as men and as members of one world.

By world-wide and improved communication men will be enabled to exchange spiritual and not merely material goods. In the realm of science any society can import ideas and add them to its existing stock, thus increasing its intellectual resourcefulness. Artistic and aesthetic experiences cannot, like ideas, be removed as they stand from one mind to another. But they can be grafted and absorbed, and thus bring a new strain from abroad into every indigenous culture.[22]

All personal and national achievements and all the monuments of human genius will be at every man's call. This varied community of possession will be the corrective of sameness. For the common treasure, thanks to the works of humane culture, will include diverse ideas and ideals, dreams and imaginings, and a vast range of concrete experiences. The freedom of the aesthetic experience enables it to wander through the infinite realm of ideals. It may be as visionary as it likes, provided only its visions be vivid and meaningful. It will be constantly augmented by new records of new experiences, for innovation is of the very essence of art, just as novelty is of the essence of experience. Thus every man will be presented with inexhaustible alternatives; and the wider the choice, the less likely it is that any man's choice will be the same as any other man's.

Global culture, rightly fostered and rightly enjoyed, will make a world in which men, despite their similar means, may preserve their different ends, and despite their similar ends, their different means, within a broad frame of harmony. It will enrich that personal life which the moral organization of society leaves to the guidance of its own taste. There will be a cross-fertilization and an overlapping of cultures, with varying degrees of uniformity but no identical or static culture. Men and nations will still enjoy the adventure of mutual discovery, but without conquest. They will contrive to speak of different things in different languages, with partial understanding eked out with sympathy and tolerance, and so without loss of that residual mystery which gives men their integrity and uniqueness.

CHAPTER SEVEN

Education and World Citizenship

ALL human institutions—moral, political, legal, and economic—reside in the minds of the men who live under them. But only a small fraction of this institutional-mindedness is, at any given time, above the level of consciousness; and if by some accident all the members of an institution should for a time lapse into dreamless sleep, the institution would still exist, in their latent habits, capacities, memories, and attitudes, and in the relations of these to one another. Education is the process by which these interrelated dispositions are acquired.

Culture originally meant not the products of cultivation but the process of cultivation, not the crop but the raising of the crop—the fertilization of the soil, the selection and sowing of the seed, and the care of the growing plant. This second process is now called education. Culture will then mean the wardrobe which a member of society has at his disposition; education will mean the dressing of him, including the selection of what is most becoming and useful, and the fitting of it to the individual's figure.

The basic task of education is to maintain cultural continuity in successive generations of individuals. The fundamental fact for education is that in the individual human life it is begun over and over again. Society is composed of individuals, and yet each individual starts as nothing and as nobody and ends as a member of the society to which he belongs, having acquired in the course of living that mode of living which prevails among the more or less finished individuals by whom he is surrounded. Society perpetually replaces its human materials and shapes them for their places.

Man's birthday clothes consist of potentialities, embracing a set of reflexes and capacities which on being presented with the appropriate stimuli are translated into action, and from action into dispositions. Having been acquired, these dispositions determine the individual's responses to new stimuli; and these responses result in new dispositions, which again determine his subsequent responses, up to and including that last act of life which is called his dying breath. He has learned to live, and finally to die, by living. Each lesson learned provides the conditions, and prescribes the manner, of his learning more.

All education is training. It is meaningless to say that one kind of thing learned is doing, for there is nothing else that is learned. It is meaningless to say that one way of learning is to learn *by* doing, for there is no other way of learning. Education is learning to walk by walking, to talk by talking, to name by naming, to handle by handling, to observe by observing, to remember by remembering, to think by thinking. It is also idle to speak of doing as distinguished from what is done. Everything is a doing of something, so that whenever one learns to do one learns *what* to do. And at the same time one learns how to do it —that is, a specific manner of doing it; and also how to do it oneself—that is, some unique way of doing it which reflects one's own personal history and idiosyncrasies.

There are various subdivisions of education which, although overlapping, will serve to indicate its many-sidedness and all-pervasiveness. There is what is called "formal education," which is the education conducted in a special social institution designed for the purpose—a school or college—and by the special profession of teaching. This kind of education is ordinarily given during the early part of the life cycle, so that it may prepare the way for the other kinds of education; namely, self-education, functional education, and education by publicity.

In self-education the individual is his own teacher, choosing what he shall learn and how he shall learn it. The precise point at which this begins cannot be determined, but it is clearly a part of formal education to endow the individual with the initial equipment required for his future self-education. Functional education comprises what the individual learns for and from his role in life; that is, his place in the social division of labor. It gives him the tools of his trade. Each individual, over and above becoming a mature man, becomes also a butcher, a baker, a candlestick maker, a citizen, a janitor, a poet, a mechanic, a plumber, a fireman, a lawyer, or a businessman engaged in some particular form of business; he has to be prepared to exercise the function, and is in turn taught by the experience which its exercise yields. In the case of the latter, the educational product may be said to be incidental rather than designed. This is what is sometimes spoken of as the school and the lesson of life. The function which the individual exercises may be chosen as congenial, in which case it is called his vocation, in the sense of calling; it may be his second choice, when it is called his avocation; or he may have to be hired to do it, in which case it is called his livelihood or job.

The fourth type of education—education by publicity—comprises what the individual learns from newspapers, books, speeches, radio, theater, or monuments of art. These are forms of communication addressed to the public; that is, promiscuously to all who have the capacity to understand them, more or less, and the inclination and means to give them their attention.

There are several further distinctions which apply within all areas of education—misleading if taken too rigidly, but useful as revealing the amplitude and complexity of the subject. The first of these distinctions is that between liberal and illiberal. There is no such thing as education which is purely liberal or purely illiberal. It is a question of degree and emphasis. Education is liberal in proportion as it fits the individual to live a human life, in that preferred sense of the term which is sometimes indicated by the words "humane," "humanity," or "humanistic."

A second distinction is that which is based on a division of human nature into intellect, will, and body. Education which enables a man to form true judgments is sometimes called instruction. Education which forms a right will is called moral education. Education which is designed to create a healthy and strong body is called physical education. Man is not thus divisible in any sense of separation. The exercise of the intellect requires a will to think and a love of truth. A well-formed will requires intelligence. Both intellect and will are, humanly speaking, embodied, and require a fund of physical energy, a normal functioning of physical organs, and an acquisition of physical skills. Human conduct is an activity of the total organism. In Greek antiquity this indivisibility was recognized in educational theory and practice. In more recent times there has been an excessive emphasis on the intellect, and moral and physical education have, as a rule, been "extracurricular."

There is a distinction between primary and secondary sources of education—between learning from the learned, and learning from the original data of nature or life. There is a temporal distinction between learning from the past and learning from the present. There is a highly important distinction between education that is repetitive and education that is innovating. The former corresponds to the distribution of consumer goods of the accepted model, and preserves the social inheritance; the latter distributes capital goods with which successive generations of men can produce better consumer goods and thus contribute to progress.

The present discussion will thread its way through this maze, with special attention to those aspects of education which have a significant relation to the postwar world.

The conditions which have increased the range, the ease, and the diversity of human intercourse must have profound effects upon education—whether for better or for worse depends on what men do with this intercourse. Never before in human history has education been convicted of crimes so great; never before have men looked so eagerly to education as a power for good. The processes by which dispositions are implanted may implant any kind of disposition; the shaping of plastic minds may result in evil-mindedness or right-mindedness, in true beliefs or in false, in wills humane or inhumane. All we can safely affirm is the magnitude of the educational force which is now placed at man's disposal to use or to abuse.

The present compactness and interdependence of the human world touches three educational questions: Who or what shall do the educating? Who shall be educated? What shall be the content of their education? These questions are interrelated, but they should not be confused.

Everything that is done internationally suggests international agencies designed for the purpose. In education, as elsewhere, this agency may be annexed to national agencies, public and private, and achieve the exercise of its international function by a meeting of minds, as exemplified by the conferences of ministers of education and representatives of departments of state which have been recently held in London, or by international congresses of teachers or students and unofficial educational leaders. But when conferences and congresses meet at regular intervals and develop their own administrative personnel, they tend to become institutions, such as the proposed permanent office, bureau, or council of international education to be built into the broader framework of a general world organization.[1] Such agencies proliferate and subdivide, creating subagencies to deal with special problems, such as the exchange of students and teachers or the distribution of educational materials.

Those who advocate international agencies for education are prompted by their occupational bias to think first of formal education; that is, of schools, colleges, and universities; but they are also alive to the new opportunity created by improved communication. The World Radio University, through its short-wave radio station WRUL, has for some years served as an educational channel by which all parts of the world and the major races of mankind can be instantly reached from a single source. The press with its international circulation and its far-flung corps of foreign correspondents brings news from everywhere to everywhere. When there is space again for the materials of peace, books, magazines, and films will be transported easily and quickly by steamship or by plane.

Television already enables Americans to see the conquest of Iwo Jima the day after it occurs, and will extend to the ends of the earth the lessons taught by pictures.

In short, the agencies of international education are ready at hand, or in immediate prospect. There remain, however, two further questions—to whom shall education be given, and in what shall the education consist?

International education implies that education shall be world-wide, given to everybody with everybody's help. It means that it is to the interest of all men that all men should receive at least a minimum of education. It means that there is a human right to education—a universal claim, to be universally recognized. This claim finds expression in the international concern for the education of "backward areas"; in the international campaign against illiteracy; and in educational relief and rehabilitation where educational facilities have been destroyed by war— as symbolized by Louvain at the close of the last war and today by Warsaw and Nanking. This does not imply that one nation shall be educated by another nation, or by some international force drawn from all nations, but rather that all nations shall help each nation to educate itself.

There remains the third question, and unless this is answered the answers to the others are of little avail. Having the purpose of educating everybody and having the facilities, in what shall everybody be educated? How shall the idea of internationality affect the content of education? We are at this point like a man standing in front of a microphone having the intention and the means of saying something to all the world, but pausing for a moment because he has not yet decided what to say.

To review the whole content of instruction in the light of internationality would far exceed the scope of the present chapter, and the capacity of the writer. It must suffice to present a few broad and scarcely debatable considerations. Happily, the requirement of economy will for some years to come call for adaptation rather than for radical reconstruction, and for the reorientation of old subjects rather than for the creation of new ones.

Mathematics, and the physical sciences and technologies, contribute to internationality through their nonnationality or neutrality. Their subject matter consists of a system of abstract relationships common to all nature; and of nature itself, which is common to all nations. It is desirable that this should be alluded to in the teaching of these subjects, so as to dispose the minds of students both to their universality and to their infinite human usefulness. They should also serve as lessons in theoretical rigor; that is, in the fidelity of conclusions to evidence. And like all subjects, they should be so taught as to convey both an appreciation of their values and a recognition of their limitations. The student should learn in the scientific classroom, and not merely from the teacher of a rival subject, that the good which science does depends on what is done with it by the human will; and that if science is to contribute to the peaceful and fruitful organization of mankind, it must serve under the supreme command of morality.

There are certain branches of instruction, called the social sciences, which embrace internationality within their content. Human geography extends men's acquaintance with the surface of the earth from the familiar regions where they live to distant and strange places, in order that these may become less distant and less strange.

It creates a map and image of man's terrestrial domain which may be carried in the mind and referred to at will. Descriptive anthropology and sociology depict the customs, manners, and the diverse families of the one great human family.

From history men learn of the life of mankind throughout recorded time, and of the interrelation of groups and nations. History must be honest and accurate, free from national prejudice and wishful thinking. But the rigor of historical teaching and research is not contradicted by its preoccupation with men's supreme concerns. It is of the essence of history that it should be selective. It must be the history of something—and not a mere assemblage of human events and their causes. It is possible to examine with equal scrupulousness the history of monarchs, dynasties, and courts, or of battles and campaigns, or of men's beliefs, or of the conditions of the common people. It so happens that with their growing mastery of techniques of fact-finding, historians have turned more and more in the direction of social and intellectual history. The reason is that the answers which history gives will depend on the questions which the historians ask; and what historians ask will, in turn, properly reflect the focus of interest on the part of the public whom they serve. When thoughtful and responsible men, obedient to the moral impulse of the day, are curious about the rise and decline of civilization, about global interdependence and the causes of war and peace, about the causes of the present great catastrophe and the hope of preventing its recurrence, they will turn to the historians; and if the historians do not have the correct answers, fictions will be accepted in their place.

It is not necessary for historians to write books or offer courses on international history. No doubt the balance needs to be redressed and gaps need to be filled in order to overcome a provincial emphasis—there is need, for example, of more history of Russia and China. But it would be still better both for the public mind and for the subject of history if historians introduced an international outlook and background into *all* that they write and teach. Their readers and students would then be rid of the illusion of isolationism. They would then see Greek history, American history, or English history as a set of local events interacting with a wider human environment; the history of the twelfth century or the eighteenth, or any other century, as a phase of the development or retrogression of human unity; the past as composed of diverse tributaries converging on the present.

The process of history is both repetitive and nonrepetitive. Every historical event resembles the past in some respects; but is at the same time novel in other respects, and unique when taken in all respects. There is a value in the sameness of history: it enables men to apply the lessons of the past to the problems of the present; and there is comfort in the thought that a present evil, or worse, has happened before. There is no better cure for pessimism than a close inspection of "the good old days." And there is a value, also, in the uniqueness of history. It proves that defeats need not be repeated; that problems old and new can be solved by invention; and if not solved today, then in time—in the limitless fecundity of time. Thus history is the great teacher of patience; not passive patience which suffers long, but active patience, which perseveres for as long as it may take and is willing to strive for a good which only remote posterity will enjoy.

There are certain branches of knowledge which serve the interest of internationality more directly. Learning of physical nature from the physical sciences, of human nature from the sciences of man, and of reality at large from the philosophers—these subjects address themselves to the problems of human organization, including that last step of human organization which is organization on a world-wide scale. They are the sciences which correspond, one to one, with the major human institutions, each of which has a specific purpose within the common purpose of morality. Hence they are moral sciences. Those who engage in them will, consciously or unconsciously, measure social organization by its moral end. If consciously, then they learn that end from that branch of philosophy which is called moral philosophy. If unconsciously, then they inherit it with the literature of their subjects, or imbibe it from the spirit of their times. These sciences or studies are politics, law, and economics, together with the constructive, rather than the merely descriptive, parts of psychology and sociology. It were better if they made their moral end explicit, instead of leaving it to their readers and students, who, pursuing other studies as well and therefore taking a rounder view of the matter, must teach it to their teachers.

Taken as a project rather than a tendency or a vision, global unity is a work of organization. How shall men achieve a common polity and a common system of law beneficent to all mankind? How shall they produce and distribute material goods on a world-wide scale and with a view to the maximum of human welfare? How shall they live together with the least friction, with the least offense to human self-respect, and with the greatest spirit of mutual helpfulness? This is what learners may now expect to learn from those who are learned in the social sciences, and what the learned must be prepared to give. Such knowledge can no longer be considered the exclusive concern of technical experts called diplomats. With the growth of human interdependence and the extension of polity, law, and economy across national frontiers, foreign policy is the business of every citizen; or in other words, all policy becomes domestic.

The remainder of the accepted curriculum of instruction consists of those studies commonly referred to as the "humanities." They embrace language and literature, the fine arts, and religion. They embrace history insofar as history deals with the humane culture of the past; and philosophy insofar as this is taken as self-expression and speculation rather than as science. Emphasis on the humanities is taken as a mark of "liberal education." Any discussion of education that did not examine this subject would, in these days, be taken as a fraudulent disappointment of legitimate expectations.

The subject is confused by the accidents of history and of departmental rivalries. To rid ourselves of these and reach a conclusion on the merits of the subject, we must begin not with a list of subjects which claim to be liberal and humanistic, but with the general meaning of that good thing which we call by these flattering names. Having the standard, we can then apply it to the subjects.

President Eliot of Harvard University took a step in this direction when he attempted to divorce the purposes of a liberal college from the prescribed study of the ancient classics. He was willing to judge not only the classics but also science, for which he desired to make a larger place, by the extent to which it formed a certain kind of man, whom he described as follows:

He is not to be a weak, critical, fastidious creature, vain of a little exclusive information or of an uncommon knack in Latin verse or mathematical logic; he is to be a man of quick perceptions, broad sympathies, and wide affinities; responsive, but independent; self-reliant, but deferential; loving truth and candor, but also moderation and proportion; courageous, but gentle; not finished, but perfecting.[2]

The idea of humanity, in its application to education, means the development of man, in both the generic and the qualitative sense. Education should prepare a man for the general and common vocation of manhood, and not merely for the special requirements of an occupation. Needless to say, the two overlap, especially as it is one of the attributes of manhood to have an occupation. But there are two ways of approaching this overlapping area: it may be considered in terms of the man, as making the most of himself; or in terms of the occupation, as being best served by certain specified qualifications.

The development of man in the qualitative sense means the development of his peculiarly human attributes—his reason, his imagination, his taste, and his freedom of choice. Here we pass from humanity to liberality. Freedom of choice requires a knowledge of alternatives, and the capacity to weigh them against one another. It requires a capacity to contemplate alternatives as ends yet unrealized; that is, as imagined possibilities. And there is more freedom in the choice of ends than in the choice of means, since the end once chosen prescribes the narrower region of its means and excludes the means to opposing ends. Thus in youth a man can, if humanely educated, choose from among all ends with all their varying means; whereas in later life he is committed by the use which he has made of his past freedom. It is quite true that the individual's choice of ends is largely dictated by his possession of their means, as well as by the limits of his capacity. But the relief of the individual from the narrowing effect of circumstance—his opportunity, including his opportunity to be educated—is the business of other social agencies, political, legal, and economic. Education must take the man with such resources as nature and society have given him, and provide him with the maximum freedom to develop the one and utilize the other.

It is sometimes said that liberal education educates for leisure, and other education for work. But this is a dangerous phrasing of the matter. The student is only too ready to accept the gospel of leisure, and may begin to practice it at once. Leisure is easily confused with inaction and idleness. There is no rewarding thing in human life that is effortless. Man was not designed to be like the lily which neither toils nor spins, and when he assumes this role, he cuts but a sorry figure. Leisure in the humanly praiseworthy sense consists not in rest and relaxation, which have their justification only as compensations of effort past or future; but in doing with its own appropriate form of effort what one chooses to do, and in doing it for its own sake rather than under the compulsion of ulterior motives.

All subjects can be humanely and liberally taught, and there is no subject that can be guaranteed to be liberal and humane, however it is taught. Pedantry in the so-called humanities is no more humane than the crassest utility in science, pure or applied; and pedantry is not even useful. But there are, nevertheless, differences in the degree to which different subjects lend themselves to liberal and humane uses. Thus, other things being equal, pure science is more humane and liberal than technology, because it leaves the mind free to choose the applications. The social sciences are more liberal and humane than the physical sciences, insofar as they equip a man for life as a whole and not merely for that part of it which consists of the control of his physical environment. History and philosophy are more humane and liberal than either physical or social science, because in their different ways they introduce a man to his total universe and present him with the maximum range of options.

As for the humanities proper, to describe them as "useless" is to deliver them into the hands of their enemies. It is a mistake for the proponents of anything to call attention to what it is not—the opponents can be trusted to attend to that. Taken for what they have positively contributed to life, the humanities—literature, the fine arts, and religion, together with history and philosophy—are humane and liberal because they call attention to what is superlatively human—that is, to the monuments and masterpieces of genius—and because they focus attention on ends and intrinsic values rather than on means, facts, and causal relations.

Liberal education in the broad social sense means that institutions are for men and not that men are for institutions. It means that men are not to be forced into a Procrustean social bed, but made room for in a flexible social order that shall accommodate itself to their advancing freedom of choice. In the broader global sense, liberal education means that international institutions shall be so fashioned as to serve this purpose of freedom for all men, either directly or through their domestic institutions, the latter being relieved of the fears and harsh constraints of war, and being enabled through co-operation to serve their several peoples more generously. It means that all men will draw from their common past and from one another, by exchange and understanding, visions, insights, and alternative goods which will attract and amplify their choice. It means that having acquired a margin beyond their animal necessities and having learned to dominate their human machines, all men shall in increasing measure live that humane life which has hitherto been only an unfulfilled promise or the rare privilege of the few.

The most important part of education, and the most neglected, is moral education. Everybody pays lip service to its importance but hesitates to practice it. Only preachers and parents have the courage to admit that they engage in this kind of educating; and the preachers try to pretend that they are not "preachers," while the parents try to sit at the feet of their children.

A superficial reason for this hesitation to engage in moral education is its supposed violation of the code of modesty. It may be assumed that the teacher knows somewhat more than his students, or at least knows it a day or so ahead; and this is, as a rule, welcomed rather than resented by the students. There should be no objection, therefore, to recognizing that a teacher of morality knows more about morality than a student of morality. But the role of teacher is here associated with what he is rather than with what he knows; and people, including students, do not like to associate with their betters, especially when their betters admit that they *are* better. Nor is this role of self-righteousness palatable to the teacher himself, whose code of manners inclines him to disclaim superiority.

But a teacher of hygiene need not be healthier than his students, provided he knows his subject. The unwillingness to teach or to learn morality may rest on the denial that morality is really a subject of which some may know more and others less. It may reflect a moral skepticism, an unfounded but widespread belief that moral statements are purely personal; and that to teach them is therefore an indecent exposure of the teacher's privacy and an intrusion upon the privacy of the student. But good and right have a meaning, and in terms of that meaning some things are good and right, others evil and wrong; some behavior conduces to happiness, and other behavior to unhappiness; some forms of social organization promote rights, and others violate them. These are propositions which can be better known by some persons than by other persons without presumption or impertinence.

It may be argued that all education has its moral effects and that moral education may therefore be left to take care of itself. What is ubiquitous and inevitable does not need to be done by art and premeditation. But this ignores the fact that the incidental effects of education on character and practice may be immoral as well as moral. Inattention to them may result in error, confusion, misconduct. Moral education, if it is to realize its end, requires that the moral should be pointed.

A further objection to moral education rests on the peculiar relation of moral knowledge to the will. It is characteristic of moral judgments that their acceptance carries with it a tendency to act. Thus if a teacher persuades a student that lying is wrong, the effect is to prevent him from lying. Moral education is thus an exercise of power, which the student may resist as depriving him of liberty, or which may be disapproved by society as inconsistent with the individual's self-determination. It is this objection, together with the charge of mendacity, which is responsible for the odium now attaching to "propaganda."

Is it possible for the friends of liberty to engage in moral education without descending to the level of their enemies?

All teaching tends to result in belief, all belief once crystallized excludes contrary belief, and all belief is incorporated in the believer's character, thus in some measure depriving him of the power to be or to do otherwise. It must be admitted that many so-called teachers are not teachers, and do not mean to be if they can help it—which they usually can. Many of the personnel of so-called educational institutions, although commonly classified as "educators," are not in the least interested in education. They are interested, for example, in physics or economics, and to some extent in training future physicists or economists, but not in preparing youth to meet the problems of life, personal and social. But whoever chooses to be a teacher must decide whether he wishes his students to become skeptics or believers; and if the latter, he must decide what predispositions are most worthy of being implanted with the probability of their becoming permanent. Even if he hesitates to implant any belief at all, this signifies that he respects the freedom of his students; and that he is willing, by example if not by precept, to implant in them at least *this respect for freedom.*

And if this predisposition should perchance coincide with the creed of his country or of organized mankind, he need not refrain from implanting it on that account; for there is no obligation of logic or morality which requires that an otherwise valid procedure should be abandoned merely because it might attach men to their own country and mankind.

Men hesitate to engage in moral education lest they be accused of indoctrination and emotional appeal. But these same men proclaim the doctrine of academic liberty as the first axiom of education. There is one doctrine which they may unreluctantly implant, and that is the creed that underlies their reluctance. They speak of love of truth and respect for facts as though love and respect were not emotions. There is one passion which they need not hesitate to excite—that passion which causes them to suspect passion and to deplore emotional infection. There is only one way of disinfecting education, and that is by the infectiousness of the scholar's devotion to learning, and to the personal freedom and organization of freedoms which learning requires.

There are institutions, such as the cradle and the nursery, for those who are not yet capable of choice, and where their choice must be made for them by responsible, though now humble, adults. There are other institutions, professional or sectarian, for those who have already made their choice. And there are those which are designed for youth whose choosing faculties are ripe, but who enter unarmed, unguarded, and uncommitted. In such an institution freedom should be methodically and systematically propagated by its every academic stratagem—by its symbols and its loyalties, its selection of teachers, the prescriptions of its curriculum, and the diffused quality of its atmosphere. It should be made extremely difficult, if not impossible, for the members of such an institution to remain unfree.

The cult of just freedom by which men condemn or withhold moral education is itself morality, or the greater part of it. It is a creed and a code; if people accept it, they are expected to live by it. This moral code suffers from refusing to admit that it is a code—from failure to be explicit in its adoption, and methodical in its propagation. By such mistaken scruples, or by doubt and confusion, it leaves the field open to other creeds and codes which, though they be immoral, are strong in the hold they acquire on their adherents and in the scope of their influence. The moral code of freedom and justice thus disarms itself in advance, and allows its enemies to prevail.

That unity of the world which we call peace and international co-operation is a moral unity. The institutions which embody and realize it are the moral institutions—politics, law, and economy—extended to that all-inclusiveness which their moral universality implies. These institutions reside in the minds of men, not only in their habits and ideas, but in their sentiments of approval and disapproval which make up what is called their conscience. To create this conscience on a global scale is the contribution of moral education to international institutions.

This so-called conscience of mankind consists of a resolve and a passion residing in each individual man, having as their object the harmonious happiness of all men. This is an edifying platitude. It means that if mankind is to achieve a certain kind of world, they must want it; those in positions of power and influence who speak for other men with other men's consent must want it; citizens of the world, in their capacity of control, must want it. There must be a widespread and dominant will, which is *for* peace and *against* war; *for* happiness and well-being and *against* misery; *for* the happiness and well-being of all men and *against* the happiness and well-being of the few at the expense of the many. This will must be steady and strong enough to hold out for as long a time as may be necessary to overcome the obstacles in its path. It must have that quality of courage by which the will is strengthened rather than dismayed by obstacles.

The world-wide intercourse among men facilitates the formation of such a will, but only provided it is employed for that rather than for some opposing purpose, by all the educational agencies of family, church, school, press, and public utterance.

Men are now receptive to this moral education on the global scale, by virtue of their vivid experience of human interdependence proved by the disastrous consequences of war. But the fundamental appeal of moral education is to that part of human nature which is variously called by the names of sympathy, compassion, fellow feeling, or humanity; and which is excited in one man by another regardless of the differences which divide them.

This is a fact about human nature, and no less a fact because it is a morally helpful fact. Even in the midst of war men have sometimes to be goaded into hostility or threatened with death to prevent their fraternizing. The common soldier wavers somewhere between the detestation of his enemy and the feeling that he is a poor devil like himself. A wounded American soldier said to his doctor, "Except when I see him over the sights of my gun, Jerry is good enough for me."

Between the politicians, lawyers, and economists on the one hand and the cynics on the other we forget the extent to which the present war is a resentment of cruelty. An American air pilot is quoted as saying:

I could stand idly by and see every painting by Rembrandt, Leonardo da Vinci, Michelangelo thrown into a bonfire and feel no more than a deep regret, but throw one small, insignificant Polish urchin on the same bonfire and, by God, I'd pull him out or else. I fight quite simply for that and I cannot see what other reasons there are. . . . Someday an American doughboy in an American tank will come lurching into some small

Polish, Czech or French village and it may fall to his lot to shoot the torturers and open the gates of the village jail. And then he will understand.[3]

The new arts of communication have enlarged and vivified the spectacle of human cruelty and of human misery. Scarcely a sparrow falls that we do not read about it, and see pictures of its shattered form. To feel compassion for the man who falls among thieves we do not have, like the Good Samaritan, to journey and come where he is; his mishap comes to us where we are. We cannot easily insulate ourselves against the pangs of pity. The man in the public conveyance who explained that he held a newspaper before his face because he couldn't bear to see women standing will now find things there depicted that are still more difficult to bear.

Men have other ways of avoiding the pangs of pity even when they must face the spectacle of human misery. They may take it as an epic and enjoy the bloody history of war for its tragic splendor—as in the Homeric fall of Troy. Or they may find it picturesque, and jest about the headhunters of Borneo. But the news of human misery now comes in too fast and in too large amounts to permit its being translated into poetry, and it comes home too close to seem funny or picturesque. And the means of prevention are too ready at hand to permit an escape from responsibility.

It is true that the springs of pity dry up, and that sympathy palls. It is true that the presence of a fellow man may excite antipathy as well as sympathy. It is true that sympathy may be ill-timed and misplaced. But this proves only that the right excitement of sympathy is an art—the art, namely, of moral education. It has been said of the Germans that they knew how to "organize sympathy." [4] The party of peace and justice should know how to organize it —how to evoke and direct it, when to subordinate it to righteous wrath, and how to reintroduce it into those forms of organized activity which have done so much to deaden it.

The cynicism of mankind—the ironical smile with which any reference to human fellow feeling is likely to be greeted —is largely due to organization. The work of the world unites men and then divides these unities against one another. Hence a man engaged in business, law, or politics is largely engaged in defeating the hopes and efforts of other men. Trained to do this in his office at least six days of the week, he is disposed to say, "This is life. This is human nature." He leaves humanity to his wife, or the priest, or the moralist, accepting it indulgently if it keeps away from the forum and the market place. And the same man who has spent most of his waking hours being ruthless can yet be kindly in his unorganized relations and in his manners.

Humanity cannot be achieved by organization if organization is to suppress humanity at its root; namely, the kindly impulse to help a fellow man in trouble rather than take advantage of his trouble. All men are more or less in trouble all the time. But men are schooled to ignore this fact, and to see others only as members of a rival organization. The kindly impulse is not destroyed. But while it remains as a part of primary human nature it is overlaid by a secondary human nature. It has no stimulus to evoke it, except in times of catastrophe when the degree of human suffering and its afflicting all alike suddenly changes the face of things, and when men suddenly become men again—poor, struggling, frustrated, disappointed, pain-suffering mortals. Then the heart leaps up and goes out to them.

So the problem of moral education touches all the organized enterprises of life, and makes it imperative to humanize every contact and relationship in the office, the factory, the party, the school, the family, and the church. Each, despite the fear of being thought sentimental or lacking in reticence, must uncover his own humanity and thus invite the humanity of others. He must have the courage to be human even at the risk of being thought unprofessional or unbusinesslike.

Sympathy in itself is not a mere feeling. It may incite to remedial action. It contributes to moral knowledge as well as to the moral will; for it is by sympathy that we experience the lives of others in their inwardness and recognize their likeness to our own. Sympathy is the only basis of the Golden Rule, as affording both evidence of its truth and a motive for its translation into deeds.

That part of education which is assigned to school, college, and university is a small fraction of education, and most of it touches only a small fraction of society.

Although so large a part of education is the education of the general public outside or after formal schooling, agencies expressly devoted to education make no place for it except in an obscure corner labeled "adult education," or "extension courses," or "correspondence schools," and often viewed with condescension, if not with contempt, by the highest-ranking teachers in the highest-ranking institutions. Such a teacher sticks to his books, his classroom, or his laboratory, while most of the world's education, including his own, goes on elsewhere. The mind of the college graduate, both in its content and in its manner of proceeding, is scarcely distinguishable from that of the non-college-graduate after both have been exposed to the weather of experience and publicity. Two graduates of different colleges who enter business will develop a sameness of outlook which penetrates their minds more deeply than the difference of their schooling. Two graduates of the same college, one of whom is a constant reader of the *New York Herald Tribune,* and the other of the *New Republic,* will have their academic sameness largely obliterated by their journalistic difference.

The agencies of publicity have been vastly multiplied in their range and effectiveness, and in their claim on the time and the attention of mankind. Books, magazines, and newspapers are manufactured and distributed in immense volume; the air is full of messages winging their way through space from sender to receiver; speakers address audiences with the aid of loud-speakers; pictures abound in the press and on the screen; and the average man is not too busy or too preoccupied to listen, read, and look. He is not compelled to do so, but it is the business of these agencies to tempt as well as to address him. It is customary to regard this vast elaboration of publicity as one of the major benefits of civilization enjoyed by an advanced country such as the United States. We are not, however, unaware of its dangers and its evils. Much of it is commercially motivated, and no more veracious than it pays to be, or than the law requires. Much of it is based on the economy of mass production and must be adapted to mass consumption and to mass appeal.

There are several ways in which the educational values of publicity can be guarded. One way is by a sort of food and drug act that prohibits the dissemination of specious or noxious ideas; another is by government ownership and operation of the channels. These political methods are limited by civil liberties, and by the general hesitation to place the making of public opinion under the control of those very authorities which should be its servants. Another way is to place channels of publicity at the disposal of teachers or educational institutions whose disinterestedness is above suspicion. But this way, while it is good so far as it goes and should be extended, does not go a long way. It does not compete successfully for the public attention with programs artfully baited for the purpose, and providing entertainment rather than instruction and edification.

The mind of the public is thus assailed by seductive appeals, on high grounds or on low; by opinions, honest and dishonest; and by honest opinions of every variety on every question. There is little likelihood that in a country devoted to free enterprise and free expression this flood will ever be controlled at its sources. Hence the importance of teaching the victim to swim or equipping him with a life belt. In an age of promiscuous and wholesale publicity it becomes a first duty of institutions designed for education to teach a man how to make up his own mind in a world in which there are so many agencies eager to make it up for him. Men should be taught sales resistance in a world of salesmanship. They cannot and should not be taught to believe nothing, but to be, as a wise writer of the seventeenth century put it, "judiciously credulous." [5] They should be taught to know the facts from the news; to distinguish knowledge from opinion, and names from calling names. They should learn to gather opinions from various sources, and so correct the one-sidedness by many-sidedness. They should be taught to be something more than literate in an age which caters to literate illiteracy; to be originators, and not mere sounding boards or transmitters. They should be enabled to serve society and themselves as centers where opinion pauses for reflection; rolling ideas gather no thought. In a word, men need to be taught how to *use* their publicity well, lest their minds be empty for lack of it, or become the mere passive products of its impact.

The modern agencies of publicity are world-wide in their range and power. The sender is anywhere, the receiver is everywhere. The content is the more voluminous and the more confusing. It is increasingly less likely or desirable that its production should be controlled; and there is a correspondingly greater need that the individual should be saved from its overwhelming effects. Education has a new duty to develop and cherish the thinking, discriminating, scrupulous individual whose influence is potentially magnified at the same time that his integrity is more gravely menaced.

The mind which can be educated can be re-educated. In fact, all education is re-education. No education begins at the beginning. It starts with a mind already predisposed, and works with old dispositions in order to create new. Never has there been more unanimous testimony to the power of education. The evils of Nazism and Japanese militarism are commonly attributed to the deliberate molding of minds by schooling and by publicity. And yet by a strange inconsistency we regard these products of education as unalterable. And at the same time that we despair of re-educating others we speak confidently of re-educating ourselves.

The difficulties of re-educating a nation are immense. The character of a nation has innumerable roots, in the shape of all its institutions, in its literature, its symbols, in the meanings which all the familiar objects of life have acquired, in the loyalties which bind its members together. All these forces have combined over the years to make the German or the Japanese what he is. They have made Germans Nazis, and they have made Japanese militaristic. It is absurd to suppose that Nazism is not German [6] and that militarism is not Japanese. Nor is either of these products exceptional and sporadic. The great majority of the people of these nations who have lived during the last few decades are deeply imbued with these cults, many of them during their more impressionable years.

But these very complexities provide also a ground of hope. There are many avenues of approach; and there are many individuals—rising generations of individuals as yet unformed, and others who have suffered martyrdom, or disillusionment, or the bitterness of failure.

Re-education starts with men's given dispositions as the condition of any effective appeal. These given dispositions are acquired forms of inherited, biological traits, so that in appealing to them one is appealing at one and the same time to nature and to culture. The anthropologists and sociologists are right, therefore, in saying that re-education begins with a cultural diagnosis.[7] This is a difficult but not impossible task.

Some of the answers are evident and generally accepted. The German looks to his institutions to compensate for his weaknesses and protect him against them. Being docile, he submits to leaders and makes a virtue of obedience. Lacking individual self-reliance, he looks for self-respect in collective action and in social status. Afraid of his softness, he subjects himself to a cult of brutality and discipline. Afraid of feeling, he substitutes method. Dr. F. W. Foerster tells a story of a German who left his dying mother with the parting injunction not to forget, before she died, to wind the clock. It is reported of a German surgeon that when he operated on a child without an anesthetic, he explained his indifference to the child's pain by pointing out that he was securely bound.[8] These Germans had succeeded in anesthetizing themselves to pity by their worship of routine and technique; and so by a profound inversion of values they forgot that routine and technique have no rational purpose but to make men happy and save them from suffering.

Afraid of that cosmopolitanism which he had himself so notably attained in the late eighteenth century, the German subordinates culture to the state. Rejecting the objective standards of truth, beauty, and utility, he adopts a subjective morality, and relieves himself of personal responsibility by merging his subjectivity into that of race and nation. Thus his method, mechanisms, and insensibility are invested with a romantic glow and a sense of profundity.

The character of Japan appears to be more elemental, though this is no doubt in large measure an effect of distance and ignorance. Germany, having shared the history of Europe and of Christendom with its opponents, is divided against itself and suffers from inner conflicts which suggest the concepts and cures of mental pathology. Japan has a more integral inheritance. Its code is essentially the warrior's code, sanctioned by tribal gods and clannish solidarity. Watching the struggles for power among European nations, and biding its time, Japan borrowed their techniques but not their humanitarian scruples. Science, industry, and all the practical arts became the instruments not of welfare, but of military conquest and Japan's self-appointed destiny.

In such national characteristics as these, together with

the common human nature always lying at their root, and the pride and emotional solidarity felt by all nations, re-education must look for the initial springs of action by which Germans and Japanese may be induced to change themselves and become, as we say, good neighbors in the global neighborhood; peace-loving, like ourselves, or shall we say, peace-loving as we hope to become by a continuing re-education of ourselves.

Without a faith in the educability and re-educability of all men and nations there is no hope of that world order of which we dream. This faith is quite independent of such punishments, reparations, quarantines, and controls as may atone for past crimes and insure the world against their repetition in the immediate years to come. But even these measures of prudence and justice must be considered in their long-run educational bearings; and the basic ideas of world order refer to the long run rather than the short.

The hope of the future lies in the perpetual plasticity of human nature, both original and acquired. So far as they are the effects of human capacities and dispositions, no good is inevitable, no evil is impossible; and, by the same token, no evil, such as war, is inevitable; and no good, such as peace, is impossible. The future of mankind will be decisively determined by what man makes of himself, through intelligence and institutions governed by the moral will.

With the spread of the moral standards and institutions which we call democracy, this moral will consists of the wills of individuals, brought to agreement by discussion and persuasion, and delegated to freely chosen authorities. "Every reform," said Emerson, "was once a private opinion, and when it shall be a private opinion again, it will solve the problem of the age." [9] The change in world affairs from a condition of conflict and exploitation to a condition of peace and co-operation is a reform in which every man is both reformer and reformed. It requires of each man that he shall be confident of his power to translate his private judgment, thoughtfully arrived at, and enriched by what he learns from others, into public opinion and into public policy. This public policy, in turn, will confirm and order the freedom by which it is created.

There are phases of the development of individuals and groups in which they have to be guided toward freedom. But in proportion as education takes effect, those who learn and those who teach will share the same freedom under just institutions, and will work together to perfect it. This is the norm by which to condemn failure, and by which to measure successive forward steps, in the education of the citizens of one world. It does not suggest the dissemination of wisdom from on high, or any centralized system of propaganda; but a gathering of wisdom from many sources, and the enjoyment of self-determination in the making up of minds—a self-determination limited only by the wide frame of justice and by that moral will through which a just self-determination is sustained.

So conceived, as embracing formal schooling and the arts of publicity, the continuity of tradition and the novelties of invention, the discipline and furnishing of the intellect and the forming of character and taste, the gathering of facts and the stirring of imagination—and embracing all these things for all men everywhere—so conceived, the whole story of history, up to its latest and most extravagant hopes, is the story of mankind's self-education.

CHAPTER EIGHT

The Humanity of Religion and the Religion of Humanity

MEN peer as best they can beyond their earthly and mortal horizons. Religion speaks for their loftiest aspirations and their deepest and most enveloping thoughts, and puts the two together. It represents what men hope for their ideal from their knowledge of the real. Their aspirations may not be very high, or their knowledge very deep. Their conception of the ideal may be a mere projection of their appetites, and their conception of the real a mere acceptance of appearances. When this is the case, religion is said to be primitive. Advanced religions unite the insights of seers and moralists with the refinements of science and metaphysics. Taken as a union of the maximum of truth with the maximum of goodness, religion is the crowning achievement of humane culture.

Philosophy, like religion, deals both with the order of value and with the order of being. But whereas philosophy is a theoretical pursuit, religion is belief felt and practiced. Philosophy lived becomes religion, and religion reflected upon becomes philosophy.

Religion must always contain a margin of belief over doubt and of hope over despair. But the degree of hope may descend from certitude to probability, and from probability to sheer faith; and the hope itself may be positive or negative—a hope of arrival, or a hope of escape in which the evil is so greatly dreaded that the very nothingness of its avoidance takes on the emotional quality of good.

It might seem simpler to say that religion is the worship of God. But then it becomes necessary to explain God, and this will take us back to the same two ideas. God unites the creation and control of nature with the attributes of perfection; his will is both powerful and good—an almighty power for the highest good. As for worship, the term suggests what is only a part of religious life; namely, adoration and prayer. Religion also embraces action—obedience of God's will, and guidance by his commands.

Nor is religion to be identified with the church. Religion may consist of the experience of a lonely soul, or the independent practice of a nonconforming individual. But it so happens that men usually share their religious beliefs, which then become a creed. Their collective worship then takes the form of ritual, their collective practice takes the form of a cult, and they become members of a social institution called a church.

While the whole of religious belief is two-dimensional, the union of an idea of ultimate value with an idea of ultimate reality, the name of religion is often given to either half taken by itself. The justification for this lies in the fact that most men derive both these ultimates from their religion. From their religion they acquire their idea of the universe in which they live, and from religion they acquire their idea of what it is that makes life worth living. Religion thus becomes the most important channel through which each of these ideas finds its way into the beliefs, emotions, and practice of the multitude.

Hence it is from their religion that most men today derive their *ideal* of the postwar world. In Europe and the Americas the Christian and Jewish churches have supported the cause of world unity on moral grounds. They leave to others the arguments on political, economic, and legal grounds. They leave to others the appeal to prudence, enlightened self-interest, and the fear of war; they themselves appeal to reason, conscience, and the sentiment of humanity. In the autumn of 1943, a *Catholic, Jewish, and Protestant Declaration on World Peace* [1] was adopted by one hundred and fifty representatives of these religious bodies in the United States, and distributed to over 750,-000 persons. It begins with the affirmation that "The Moral Law Must Govern World Order" and follows with six further articles:

The Rights of the Individual Must Be Assured; The Rights of Oppressed, Weak or Colonial Peoples Must Be Protected; The Rights of Minorities Must Be Secured; International Institutions to Maintain Peace with Justice Must Be Organized; International Economic Cooperation Must Be Developed; A Just Social Order Within Each State Must Be Achieved.

The Federal Council of Churches, representing different Protestant denominations in the United States, has adopted a *Statement of Guiding Principles for a Just and Durable Peace,* including the following:

As members of the Chrisitan Church, we seek to view all problems of world order in the light of the truth concerning God, man and God's purpose for the world made known in Jesus Christ. We believe that the eternal God revealed in Christ is the Ruler of men and of nations and that His purpose in history will be realized. For us He is the source of moral law and the power to make it effective.

From this faith Christians derive the ethical principles upon which world order must be based.

The Catholic Association for International Peace has issued a statement in parallel columns in which the principles of the Atlantic Charter are supported item for item from papal pronouncements, beginning with the call for "a new order based on observance of the moral law," among peoples and governments.

All these, and many similar statements,[2] agree in their demand for what one of them describes as "a new era, the era for which peoples have been longing through the centuries, the era in which nations will live together in justice and charity." [3]

In all of these statements the several religious bodies reserve their special teachings in order to emphasize their agreement on common moral principles. And they invite the agreement not only of all Christians but of the party of morality throughout the world. Thus after a broad profession of the Christian creed, the Preamble of the *Statement* of the Federal Council of Churches goes on to say:

From this faith Christians derive the ethical principles upon which world order must be based. These principles, however, seem to us to be among those which men of goodwill everywhere may be expected to recognize as part of the moral law. In this we rejoice. For peace will require the cooperation of men of all nations, races, and creeds.

Similarly, in November 1943 the National Catholic Welfare Conference issued a statement in which the following paragraph appears:

It is heartening to note the wide agreement on the moral postulates of a just peace among religious leaders, otherwise

divided by the deep cleavage of fundamental doctrinal differences. This significant and hopeful agreement has recently been
evidenced in three parallel statements on world peace issued
by American religious groups. This pattern for peace fashioned on the moral law has attracted nation-wide attention
and will, we hope, be carefully studied by all men of good
will.[4]

This moral solidarity, throughout Christendom and
reaching beyond Christendom to men of goodwill everywhere, signifies the growth of that world conscience without which international institutions can be of no avail. It
consciously links the instrumentalities of world order to
their moral end. It should not be belittled because it is
visionary and uncompromising. Let us assume that public
policy at any given time is a bargain struck between ideals
and circumstance. The level of compromise will depend
on the demands of both parties, and it is imperative that
the moral party should ask for everything in order to obtain as much as possible. Morality, through religion, its
chief popular advocate, should, like science and art, cherish and express its own purity of motive. But pure morality, unlike pure science and pure art, is easily understood.
Its terms are hard, but its language is familiar. Its oversimplification of human problems and the very absolutism
of its dictates bring it within the range of the average
man, who need not be politician, lawyer, economist, psy-
chologist, sociologist, or historian in order to become its
adherent.

The issue between the old order and the new has its
religious counterpart in the difference between tribal religions and universal religions. A tribal religion worships
a god who is the partisan of the social group to which

{ 239 }

his worshipers belong in all their conflicts with rival groups each championed by its rival god. The tribal god is a god of war, not the common god of all warriors, but the god of only one of the combatants. Tribal religion is thus a divisive force in human history, and reflects its other divisive forces.

The essence of a universal religion is its equal and undiscriminating appeal to all the nations and races of earth, or to all men regardless of their nationality or race. Its god is a god of all mankind. Its offer of salvation is addressed to the shortcomings and hopes which all men have in common. Its teachings are based on the common experiences of life and death, so that every man may verify them for himself. The Christian gospel of regeneration, the Buddhist doctrine of recurrent desire and its conquest through self-denial, and the more homely wisdom of Confucianism are all universal. If there is any doubt of Mohammedanism and Judaism, it is because of the suspicion that they have not wholly freed themselves from association with the race in which they originated.

The spread of a religion such as Mohammedanism to all parts of the earth has nothing to do with its universality. Mohammedanism conquered the Near East and spread its domain to Asia, Indonesia, and Western Europe. In so far as this conquest was an Arab conquest by force of arms, it added nothing to the universality of Mohammedanism which it did not have when the Prophet uttered his first prophecies. Its One God, its allegiance to Mohammed and to the Koran as sources of wisdom, its doctrine of resurrection and predestination, are universal. Its Holy War, its pilgrimage to Mecca, and its political Pan-Arabism are tribal. Judaism became universal when the God of Israel abandoned his exclusive preoccupation with a chosen peo-

ple and became a judge of all nations, forbidding them to
lift up sword against one another. Tribal religion is not
less tribal when the tribe assumes the role of conqueror.
Religion may then fan the flame of nationalism, and add
a crowning insolence to the claims of a self-appointed mas-
ter race.

Thus the classification is not clear and sharp. It is difficult to avoid a sense of proprietorship even of the universal. It has been said of the Christianization of the islands
of the Pacific that "the Catholic missionaries left no special
national stamp on their converts as the Protestants did. It
was a Congregationalist convert who greeted a Marine
with the simple statement, 'I'm a Boston Christian.'" [5]
The traditional teachings and sacred books of all religions
have some modicum of human wisdom; and all religions,
however universal their essential teachings, may resort to
war as a means of destroying the enemies of the faith.
When Mohammedanism waged "holy wars" against Christianity, Christianity responded in kind. The Crusades of
the Christian world against the Mohammedan world did
not unite the world; and the banner of the Cross under
which in the sixteenth century the Portuguese made war
on Mohammedans in Africa, Asia, and Indonesia only reinforced their predatory commercialism. [6] Religious faith,
though speaking in the name of humanity, has armed
Christians against infidels, Catholics against Protestants,
and Protestants against Protestants.

Universal religion does not imply a universal church.
In a world order which grants religious freedom, men may
differ in their use of that freedom. There may be tribal
religions, just as there may be nationalities, provided they
keep the peace. And even universal religions will have
their religious diversities reflecting differences of social

tradition, of class, and of personality. There are many ways in which men may worship, interpret, and obey a common God. The church may represent the broader community or the narrower diversity. If the former, then ritual tends to be colorless, dogma abstract, and practice indistinguishable from secular morality. If the latter, then the community tends to be forgotten, or to become a merely external conformity.

Christianity's idea of a universal church has, however, prepared the mind of Christendom for world organization, and the Roman Catholic Church is the first, and perhaps as yet the only, truly international institution. It need not be accepted as a model either for ecclesiastical or for secular organization. But it has proved the possibility of a durable and vigorous institution having its own international control, dedicated to a world-wide purpose, and drawing its members from all the peoples of the globe.

Although many warlike things have been done in its name, and although it has been the last refuge of many belligerent scoundrels, Christianity is a gospel of peace. Those who resort to conquest in the name of Christianity are taking its name in vain.

Pope Pius XII is blamed for his perpetual reiteration in season and out of the theme of peace. But he is prompted by a proper sense of his role. Acting as a spokesman of Christianity in its essential and timeless teaching, he can urge peace out of season, when it is untimely. The Catholic Church has never denied that there may be righteous wars, or that peace must be postponed until they are victoriously concluded; but that church as an organ of Christianity properly affirms that a war is righteous only when imposed by harsh necessity, or as the only present means to the ultimate goal of peace. This has nothing to do with the untimeliness of a negotiated peace which would pave the way to future war. Whether the Pope should or must exercise temporal as well as spiritual powers is debatable. But in the case of the great body of believers this double role is inescapable. A man's Christianity, while it should influence the use of his citizenship, does not release him from its obligations, or from his duty to the fellow citizens to whom he has so deeply committed himself, for better or for worse. His piety should temper, but it cannot be expected to extinguish, his patriotism. Hence Christians are found on both sides of the wars of Christendom.

To expound the agreement of the new world order with the teachings of Christianity is to traverse familiar ground. The Christian God is the God of all men, and the Christian offer of salvation applies equally to all men. A recent Catholic writer sums it up as follows:

All men, the Church teaches, were created the same, given the same rights, suffered the same by the Fall, were redeemed by the Christ in the same manner. . . . Only 15 percent of mankind are Catholic, and another 15 percent non-Catholic Christians. "Love thy neighbor as thyself," applies . . . to the 70 percent of men who are non-Christians as well as to the little minority whom we count among our own.[7]

In the teaching of Christianity man is dignified as the crowning creation of God, made in his image, and the object of his special concern. All men alike are his children, whom he loves as a father loves his children. Their relations to this Creator and Father—their disloyalty and their regeneration—constitute the central theme of the existing universe. The Christian God is essentially a God of love, and a God of justice only because love has been

{ *243* }

violated, or in order that it may be restored. The relation of love is reciprocal and all-pervasive—God loving men with a fatherly love reciprocated by their filial love, and man loving man with a reciprocal brotherly love. Add to this the cult of Mary as mother, and of Christ as bride-groom, and the saying of Jesus—"Suffer the little children to come unto me, and forbid them not: for of such is the kingdom of God"—and it is as though every strain of human tenderness has been invoked to enrich the sentiment of religious love. Christ himself, for whom this religion is named, is the symbol of human suffering and compassion, and signifies that God in order to be divine must partake of humanity.

This being so, the Christianity in Christians and in Christendom—in Central and Eastern as well as in Western Europe, in the Americas as well as in Europe, and in its scattered distribution to other continents—can be reckoned as a source of strength to those who would unite and organize mankind.

The hopes of the world now embrace a raising of the standard of living for all men everywhere. To this moral end of human welfare, Christianity now lends its powerful support. It is greatly to the credit of Christianity that it has altered its conception of human welfare to keep pace with the times. It has not been satisfied to proclaim the broad principle of brotherly love, but has assimilated the secular progress by which this principle is more positively, constructively, and effectively applied.

Christianity began with the teaching of otherworldliness, and has never abandoned that teaching. It has directed and still directs men's attention to a hereafter in which they may hope to enjoy a greater and more durable happiness than is obtainable during their mortal existence. But the emphasis has steadily shifted from the idea of eternal welfare *instead* of temporal welfare, to the idea of eternal welfare *in addition* to temporal welfare. Owing to this change, Christianity is now enabled to ally itself with all the friends of temporal welfare, asking not less but more.

Christianity has been charged with indifference to the general problem of human misery. This does not mean that Christianity has ever been without compassion; its charity and Good Samaritanism are indisputable. It was of the essence of Jesus, both his precept and his example, that he should have healed the sick, befriended the poor, and been disturbed even more by the sufferings of men than by their sinfulness. But Christian charity has seemed to be casual and superficial. The Good Samaritan happened to be passing that way as he journeyed, and saw the man who had fallen among thieves. He gave him first aid, but did not go to the root of the matter, or seek fundamental social remedies. The emphasis is placed, furthermore, not on the binding of wounds but on the attitude of charity. The parable suggests that human misery is a field for the exercise of a moral quality, instead of an evil to be removed.

This emphasis on the merit of giving rather than on the benefits received gives to Good Samaritanism a flavor of condescension. The giver gives from his abundance what he is under no compulsion to give. Charity is a kind of undeserved gratuity, like the grace of God. And it is supposed to be received with gratitude. The Christian Gospel in its primitive form thus suggests a static society in which the misery of the many is accepted as a fatality—as a part of the order of things since man's expulsion from Paradise.

It then becomes the office of religion not only to make a virtue of misery, but to reconcile men to its acceptance. Religion becomes a cure for the discontent which misery breeds rather than a cure for the misery itself. It teaches men to acept their lot cheerfully rather than to improve it.

Finally, the ready acceptance of this teaching by the fortunate few is not above suspicion. The standard of cheerful acceptance is welcomed by those who find it easiest to be cheerful. It enables them to slip through the eye of the needle merely by accepting their good fortune gratefully, by despising the goods which they have never had to do without, and by giving alms which they can easily afford. This tends to put religion on the side of the status quo, and to ally religion with those whom the status quo most richly rewards.

During the Middle Ages and the early years of the modern period Christianity kept alive the claims of humanity, and by its condemnation of usury and excessive profits did something to alleviate the effects of greed. When the Industrial Revolution greatly enlarged man's power to produce and distribute material goods, the Christian conscience was quick to sense its abuses, and prompted legal measures to prevent them. But in Protestant countries, where the new economy first established itself, Christianity exercised a divided influence. Christian socialists condemned the system as a whole, as contrary to the Christian teaching that the fruits of the earth and of human labor belong of right to all men as partners in a common enterprise. But at the same time the Protestant, and particularly the Calvinistic, emphasis on individual effort, thrift, self-discipline, and self-reliance provided a Christian sanction for the motive of selfish gain and for the accumulation of private wealth. Human misery was taken as a deserved penalty for moral weakness. Christians found themselves, by the practice of virtue and by their desire to prove themselves the elect of God, profiting at the expense of their fellow men, and accepting with pious self-approbation a widening gulf between the rich and the poor.

It is necessary to dwell on these less pleasant aspects of Christian history if we are to understand the charges of the enemies of Christianity, and the degree to which these charges have now lost their force. Without a sober recognition of the force of the indictment, it is impossible to understand the meaning of modern social revolutions and the fact that they have so often taken the form of anti-clericalism, anti-Christianity, and anti-religion. In the long run men are not willing to have their "pie in the sky by and by" if they believe that it is within their power to get it now, and within the power of society, if better organized, to increase the quantity of pie. The Communist dictum that religion is an opiate for the poor and the church an instrument of the propertied class has more than a grain of truth. Socialism in all its phases, Christian and secular, moderate and extreme, expresses the idea that there is something radically wrong with an economy that dispenses its benefits with gross inequality, and which makes the masses of mankind, including the workers, dependent on the indulgence of a few. It expresses the resolve that a religion which excuses the present system or refuses to approve its reform shall be forced to stand aside. Christian leadership no longer either excuses or refuses.

The present idea of human welfare expresses the belief that the unfortunate have a right to better conditions, not by the charity of the fortunate, but by the exertion, if needs be, of their own power; that the unfortunate, including those who by the work of their hands can only precariously obtain the bare necessities of life, have a right to unite and to profit by their greater number; and that the achievements of science and the technical arts, turned to social ends on a world-wide scale, can open to everybody a high minimum of convenience, comfort, self-development, and freedom of choice. These hopes and beliefs are now shared and proclaimed by the leaders of Christianity. Whether this signifies a change of heart and tardy acknowledgment of error, or only an unfolding and adaptation of what was already implicit in its teachings, does not much matter. The important thing is that it allies Christians, Protestant and Catholic, with socialism and capitalistic liberalism in a common social program.

The "joint proposals" put forward in 1940 by the Archbishops of Canterbury and York, the Catholic Archbishop of Westminster, and the moderator of the Free Church Federal Council representing English Nonconformists, proclaimed that "the resources of the earth should be used as God's gifts for the whole human race and used with due consideration for the needs of present and future generations." [8]

The famous *Malvern Manifesto* of the Church of England (1941) contains the following paragraph:

It is a traditional doctrine of Christendom that property is necessary to fullness of personal life; all citizens should be enabled to hold such property as contributes to more independence and spiritual freedom without impairing that of others; but where the rights of property conflict with the establishment of social justice or the general social welfare, those rights should be overridden, modified or, if need be, abolished. [9]

The same theme appears in *A Message from the National Study Conference on the Churches and a Just and*

Durable Peace issued by leaders of American Protestantism in 1942:

Any economic program which allows the quest for private
gain to disregard human welfare, which regiments human beings and denies them freedom of collective bargaining, thus
reducing labor to a mere commodity; any program which results in mass unemployment or dire poverty in mine or factory
or farm . . . is manifestly wrong. Against such evils the church
should arouse the conscience of mankind in every nation. The
church must demand economic arrangements measured by human welfare as revealed by secure employment, decent homes
and living conditions, opportunity for youth, freedom of occupation and of cultural activities, recognition of the rights of
labor, and security in illness and old age. To secure these arrangements it must appeal to the Christian motive of human
service as paramount to personal or governmental coercion.[10]

Most notable of all in their reasoned consistency and
in the pervasiveness of their influence are the pronouncements of the Vatican; reaching back to Thomistic doctrines, applied to modern conditions in Pope Leo XIII's
Rerum Novarum of 1891 and Pope Pius XI's *Quadregesimo Anno* of 1931, and subsequently reaffirmed down
to the recent Christmas messages of Pius XII. There is a
clear rejection of laissez-faire capitalism insofar as this
gives license to individual and national selfishness; a declaration that the bounties of earth are designed for all men
and all nations alike; a coupling of the right of private
property with an obligation to use it for the common
good; a recognition of the right of all men to material
goods, as an indispensable condition of their development
as free persons; an acknowledgment of the peculiar rights
of workers to enjoy the fruits of their labor and to bargain collectively; an affirmation of the duty of the state

to intervene against economic injustice, and of prosperous nations to help the less prosperous and dependent areas; a bold, unqualified defense of global economy as the only economy that will realize these ends, as the logical sequel to man's shared ownership of the surface of the earth, and as fitting the requirements of the "new order founded on moral principles." [11]

This Christian program is neither procapitalistic nor anti-capitalistic, prosocialist nor anti-socialist, procollectivist nor anti-collectivist, prolabor nor anti-labor, in any doctrinaire sense. It is equally opposed to the irresponsible selfishness of capitalism and to the forced regimentation of socialism. Judged in terms of the fundamental Christian standard, both capitalism and socialism, or a mixture of the two, are means and not ends, experiments and not dogmas. They are justified insofar as they meet two requirements: the satisfaction of human needs justly and abundantly, and the safeguarding of the development and freedom of human personality.

All the great religions face the same problem of adapting their unworldly teachings to their place in the world, and to the worldly preoccupations of their adherents. Mohammedans, Buddhists, Brahmans, and Confucians, like Christians, are men; and as men living in a physical environment, they are obliged to provide for their material needs. They have to be fed, clothed, sheltered, and protected from disease; they require tools and techniques, and means of communication and transport; they must produce and distribute industrial goods; and for all these purposes they require an economy. Christianity was born in Asia, but it grew up and spent its mature years in Europe, where the Industrial Revolution and the modernized economies also grew up. The Christians, the industrialists, and the economists were the same people. It is not strange, therefore, that Christianity should have assimilated these developments into its own development, and that it should now be prepared to implement human welfare with advancing technology and industrial organization.

Meanwhile the other great religions have been living elsewhere, in regions whose economy is primitive or obsolete. Modernization comes abruptly, and it comes from abroad, as something "European" or "Western," or labeled with the particular country of its origin. It therefore generates resistances, from local pride, indigenous culture, and attachment to tradition. Religion is often the focus of such resistances, but it gives way, either by withdrawing and making room for secular teachings, or by reinterpreting its own teachings.[12]

In the Moslem world both forms of adjustment appear. The inhabitants of the Near East need better transportation, and the level deserts lend themselves to the airplane, and to the automobile even though its horn drowns the call to prayer from the minaret; the need of capital leads to borrowing and borrowing requires the payment of interest, which was prohibited by the law of the Prophet.[13] The spread of education leads to a popular demand for the benefits of civilization, to the emancipation of women, and to a profound alteration of a social structure originally designed for nomadic peoples. The result of this clash is that the old Mohammedanism is discredited. There may develop, as in Turkey, a lay movement analogous to the agnostic liberalism and anti-clericalism of Western Europe and to the Communist cult of irreligion. But others find in the teaching of Mohammed, or in the Koran, or in the history of Moslem science, seeds of progress which reconcile the ancient piety with the modern age.

All of these changes and tensions appear in India on a scale proportional to its greater population, its philosophical genius, its agility of mind, and the great treasures of its religious literature. No religion was originally more otherworldly than Hinduism, more disillusioned, or more mystical. In no other country have the social practices sanctioned by religion been so diametrically opposed to the modern gospel of human welfare founded on the humanitarian use of science and technology. But asceticism, fatalism, mendicancy, priestcraft, the caste system, the harsh subjection of women and of the untouchables, are on their way out; and industrialization, individual opportunity, and social justice are on their way in—with the full support of men such as Gandhi and Nehru, who are notable for their piety. Indian cults are finding a way, without loss of their essential religious values, of eradicating human misery instead of thriving on it or using it as a springboard for absorption into Brahma or Nirvana.

Of all Asiatic religions Confucianism, divorced from its association with the old Chinese Empire, lends itself most readily to a scientific program of human welfare. The core of its teaching is rationalistic and utilitarian; it is individualistic and humanitarian in its ethics; it recognizes the importance of science and commerce, and the unity of mankind.[14] Chinese Taoism, sprung from the teachings of Lao-tse, has tended to become indistinguishable from the cult of personal morality. Chinese Buddhism has moved away from monkishness and asceticism toward education, social reform, and the service of mankind. Indeed, adding the influence of Communism, it would appear that the danger in China is not a resistance of religion to change, but a disappearance of religion altogether.

While in certain parts of Eastern Asia, such as Thailand, Buddhism has been an obstacle to industrialization through its negation of the motives of enterprise, in Japan, as in China, its teaching of compassion for human misery has been linked with a program of welfare. So long as the rising spirit of nationalism permitted, Japanese Buddhism developed rapidly in the direction of social reform, missionary evangelism, universality, and co-operation with the other world religions, especially Christianity. Indeed, it claimed superiority over Christianity in its freedom from dogma and its complete receptivity to the advancing truths of philosophy and science.

But in Japan universal religion has reverted or succumbed to tribal religion. Though of all Oriental countries Japan alone has overtaken and kept pace with the industrial and technological developments of the West, in Shintoism these developments are dedicated to military and nationalistic ends. The alliance of the opposite ends of the Axis was religious and not merely political or opportunistic. Shinto far surpasses the vulgar and trivial efforts of Rosenberg. Taking a primitive faith and uniting it with the worship of the Emperor, Japan has developed a truly totalitarian and imperialistic religion, which has its roots in the local soil and its effects in the wide area of expanding power. Shintoism is a superracism which claims to embrace all races within itself, and a supernationalism which offers itself as a substitute for the League of Nations.

The idea of human welfare justly extended to all men as their equal right, continuously raised to higher levels by scientific invention and improved industrial organization, is unlikely to find any religious sanction in Japan while Shintoism prevails, or in Germany until Christianity is restored.

The religions of the world present on the world-wide scale the same possibilities of conflict that have wrought such havoc in the past both within and among nations. The United Nations are pledged to solve the problem by tolerance rather than compulsion, having named religious freedom among the freedoms which they promise to respect. Since President Franklin Roosevelt was peculiarly insistent on this freedom, it may be assumed that it is to be understood in its American meaning.

Religious freedom in the United States is defined by Article VI and the First and Fourteenth Amendments of the Federal Constitution, by the constitutions of the several states, and by a series of judicial decisions in which these have been interpreted,[15] Neither Congress nor any state may establish a form of religion or prohibit its exercise; neither Congress nor any state (save possibly a few exceptions) may impose religious qualifications for public office.

The essence of this doctrine is the benevolent neutrality of the public authorities in matters of religion. The right of any group to religious freedom is, like all rights, limited by the similar rights of other groups, and by the whole system of rights, religious and nonreligious, which are embodied in the law of the land. As summarized by a recent writer, "there is a right to practice any religious principle and teach any religious doctrine which does not . . . injure the personal rights of others, nor offend the laws established by society for peace and morality." [16]

This limitation, while highly restrictive in the area of

action, is very liberally interpreted in the area of belief and worship. Even the laws against blasphemy, although they remain in the statutes of certain states, are rarely invoked.[17] The United States Constitution contains no explicit provision with respect to anti-religious propaganda, and its legal status is not precisely determined. But the profession and teaching of atheism is legal, provided it remains within the limit of "decorum." [18]

It does not follow that American democracy is irreligious, godless, or unChristian. Its provision for religious freedom implies a deep respect for religion. God has a conspicuous place in the Declaration of Independence, written as this was by men who believed in God. The Supreme Court has declared that the United States is a "Christian nation." [19] As it can scarcely fail to be, since the majority of its people are Christians, and all of its people, together with their institutions, are imbued with the Christian tradition.

The history and the logic of the doctrine of religious freedom are briefly as follows. Whereas in the Middle Ages Christendom was comparatively unified and fought extended wars against the infidel, in the fifteenth and sixteenth centuries its wars became civil wars—between Catholicism and Protestantism or between rival sects of Protestantism. The bloodshed and human misery attending the Thirty Years' War and the Puritan Revolution made a profound impression on contemporaries, similar to that created by the two World Wars of the present century. It threatened to destroy the orderly life of human society and the whole fabric of civilization. Religious toleration was advanced not as an expression of religious indifference, but as a solution of the problem of man's divided and passionate convictions. The same strength of conviction which impels the men of one faith to force it on others impels these to resist or to enforce their own faith in return. Each religion seeks to possess itself of political power as an instrument of conformity. It is a war to the death—to the death of all faiths, and to the neglect of the ends which political power is designed to serve. For polity, so the argument runs, is designed primarily to keep the peace. Its public function is to enable men's private interests to flourish without hindering or destroying one another. Religion is one of these private interests, and must, like others, conform to the code of civil polity if it is to enjoy its protection.

What is the effect of this conception of civil polity upon religion? It has been rejected, in the supposed interest of religion, on two grounds. It has been argued that if any given religious teaching is true, then it should be taught to everybody, and the teaching of opposing errors should be prohibited. But the conclusion does not follow from the hypothesis. If a doctrine is true, the way to bring about its adoption is not to prohibit the teaching of the opposite, but to produce the evidence, liberate people's minds, and allow them to choose. There is no other way; for if a man affirms a proposition because he has never heard of any other, or because he will be penalized if he affirms another, he may profess the proposition and even believe in it, but he will not know its truth. The other religious argument against religious freedom is the value of conformity. It is said that the full meaning of any religious teaching can be realized only in a society in which it is universally accepted, so that it governs all institutions and human relations: Christianity can be perfected only in a Christian community, Catholic Christianity in a Catholic community, Calvinistic Christianity in a Calvinistic community, Buddhism in a Buddhist community.

There are, however, insuperable difficulties which stand in the way of enforced religious conformity. History reveals the difficulty of creating and maintaining religious conformity even in the relatively limited and protected societies of the past. With the increase of popular education and the broadening and multiplication of human contacts this difficulty will increase. In fact, religion is not the kind of thing that *can* be enforced. All that can be enforced is *external* conformity, or the *appearance* of conformity—the attempt to enforce belief can only lead to hypocrisy. "Neither God is pleased," as John Robinson said, "by unwilling worshippers." [20] A sincere and inward piety which touches men's hearts and brings them to God has to be fostered by other means, such as education, preaching, or collective worship. Hence even those who pursue religious conformity as a goal will not invoke the force of the state, but will prefer an atmosphere of freedom—both to bring about conformity and to keep it, once created, sound at the core.

It might also be argued, and has been argued, that a Christianity which uses coercion, as did the Spanish Inquisition and the Puritan theocracy of New England, loses more in the quality of its Christianity than it gains in the number of its adherents. Such conformity as can be obtained by persecution has to be balanced against the hardening of the persecutors' hearts; and the result may well be more Christians but less Christianity. Finally, there is a gain in multiplicity, if it be granted that revelation is progressive, and that religions can learn from one another; religion is woven of many strands and, like all human insights, may be fed from many sources.

These, then, are the reasons for the freedom of religion in the world at large, under international institutions: the avoidance of religious wars and their destructiveness to all human interests, including religion; the defeat of the religious spirit itself through the corruption of the persecutor; the growth of religious truth through the resort of the mind to the evidence; the mutual enrichment of all religions through their friendly intercourse; the enjoyment by all mankind of the insight of the seers of all races and epochs; the growth of universal piety through the intercourse of all particular pieties.

Morality is, in the history of both the individual and society, commonly identified with the will of some superior—the parent, the ruler, the priest, the prophet, or some one of these taken as speaking for the will of God. Such sanctions add greatly to the force of morality, and it would be folly to refuse their support. Men are undoubtedly more *inclined* to do what is right if they are commanded to do so by a being whom they are already inclined to obey from love or fear or reverence. There remains the question whether right would still be right even if it were not so commanded. Theistic ethics says no: There is no moral obligation, no duty, no right, unless these are imposed on the human will by a higher divine will. Hence, according to this view, men who do not believe in God have no *reason* to be just and humane, or to play their parts in a social order, national or international, based on these principles.

The rebuttal of this doctrine lies within the range of any man's experience. Let him ask himself whether morality would lose its own proper and intrinsic force if God were eliminated; he will find a plain answer. Justice would still be justice, and kindness, kindness. Justice is owed to those who have claims, and kindness to those who have feelings—suffering is itself a sufficient ground for pity. Any will which is a will, having a capacity of choice, being the custodian of its own interests, and by its action helpful or hurtful to the interests of others, has duties. Any purpose creates an obligation to adopt the means to its fulfillment. One may do good to please a parent, a Sunday-school teacher, a priest, or God: but the primary intent of benefaction is to please the beneficiary.

Those who deny this must be prepared to take account of certain grave implications. In the first place, it means nothing to speak of God as a God of righteousness unless righteousness has a meaning of its own apart from God's possession of it. Nothing could be less flattering to God than to say that he is the being who can make anything right by willing it; his will is then a pure caprice, devoid of all merit save power. Nothing could be less flattering to man than to say that he is a being who obeys God no matter what God wills; his obedience is then a pure abjectness. Secondly, he who insists that morality is inseparable from theism takes ground similar to that of his dearest opponents. For Marxism has affirmed that morality is inseparable from dialectical materialism—from atheism. Both theist and atheist agree that morality is inseparable from an attitude toward God—whether acceptance or rejection. Meanwhile it is fortunate that the civil order of mankind is not obliged to attend upon the chills and fevers of theistic belief and unbelief. Jacques Maritain tells us that a society of free men must be theist.[21] If he means that being free they will become theist, that is one thing, for which there is much to be said. But to say that their code of civic freedom must await their conversion to theism is to cut off their best opportunity of arriving at that true understanding of the good which all theists must believe to be an essential part of theism.

And finally, that moral unity of the world which is now the common purpose of men who consider themselves enlightened and right-minded must for some time to come embrace both theists and atheists, and must be achieved by their united effort. The leaders of Catholic thought have gone far toward recognizing and accepting that fact. Pope Pius XII has said that "this high purpose and crusading struggle" should "enlist all unselfish and great-hearted men," and proceeds as follows:

It is fitting that in the formulation of the peace there should be assured the cooperation, with sincerity of will and energy, with the purpose of a generous participation, not only of this or that party, not only of this or that people, but of all people, yes, rather of all humanity. It is a universal undertaking for the common good, which requires the collaboration of all Christendom in the religious and moral aspects of the new edifice that is to be constructed. . . . We turn to all those who are united with Us at least by the bond of faith in God.[22]

The Pope has returned again and again to this theme of a great common cause to be achieved by the united effort of all humanity, or of all men of "goodwill"; [23] but usually with the reservation that they must believe in God—"Almighty Creator and Father of all, Supreme and Absolute Lawgiver, Allwise and Just Judge of human actions. When God is denied, every basis of morality is undermined." [24] This reservation at once defeats the universality of the appeal. Of the 70 per cent of the world population who are conceded to be non-Christian, a considerable fraction either reject God altogether or worship a God having little or nothing in common with the Christian God. These are not a mere residuum of backward people who can confidently be expected to become theists as their education and civilization advances; they embrace millions of men of goodwill, in China, in Soviet Russia, and widely distributed among the nations of Europe and America, who are familiar with modern science, who are responsive to a humane appeal, and who well understand the basic moral principles on which the new world order must be founded.

According to present plans, the kingdom of man is to be enlarged to the proportions of an empire. This does not prevent its incorporation into a kingdom of God.

The autonomy of civic morality does, it is true, stand in the way of a supernaturalism which would either ignore or despise the life of man on this planet. Earth cannot be regarded as a mere jumping-off place for Heaven; or as a mere proving ground for the development of virtues which fit man for life elsewhere. Man's mortal existence has its own values, and these values have been deepened and extended by a new sense of solidarity. The kingdom of God, however conceived, must make room for this kingdom of man.

Man's life with man together on the earth's surface is inescapable. It is a part of what is meant by man. Poets have their horizontal neighbors however high their spirits may soar in the vertical direction; saints, if they do not have wives and children, have fellow celibates and providers of their bodily needs; prophets render unto Caesar. Whether or not men are members of a kingdom of God, they are members of a kingdom of men. Whether or not religious teachings are true, it is true that their disciples form part of human society. Whatever claims may be made for the church as a divine institution, it is at least a human institution. Whether there is or is not a future life, there is at least a present life.

As human relations are inescapable, so are their laws. These impose on all religious faiths one universal requirement; namely, that their adherents shall dwell together in freedom, knowledge, and human kindness. Only cults which exalt slavery, ignorance, and inhumanity are excluded.

That man should have more than one allegiance is no new thing. There is no paradox in supposing that man's allegiance to mankind should be coupled with allegiance to a being higher than mankind. There is no obstacle to supposing that the values of faith are in some sense higher than the values of human morality. Civic morality prescribes conditions which men must fulfill, but beyond which they may rise to any heights. It is the vestibule by which all human faiths must enter; men may remain there, or pass through on their way to better-furnished chambers beyond; it is the ground floor of life from which all stairways ascend—only angels can enter Heaven by the roof or window. The morality which prescribes how mortal men shall live together fosters and does not prevent their more far-reaching outlook—back to first beginnings, forward to ultimate destiny, down to the foundations, upward from time to eternity. Society embraces the seer, but not his vision.

A complete religion has its metaphysical as well as its human dimension. Humanism and humanitarianism do not satisfy that insistent demand of the human spirit to orient itself toward the beyond—whether it be conceived as a supernatural order revealed to man by God, or the unknown which bounds the horizon of science and philosophy. The more man knows, the more humbly he is aware of the depths of his ignorance; the more familiar he is with earth, the more vividly aware he is of its littleness in the universe at large. Religion, in the full sense of the term, relates man's finitude to this infinity.

But loyalty to the kingdom of man partakes of some of the attributes of religion even in the absence of such a wider cosmic outlook. It can be a religion in the limited sense of devotion to a cause felt as greater and better than oneself. It ennobles man that he should belong to the race of men. A recent Catholic writer, speaking of man's natural dignity, has said that "if the human person be not infused and endowed with a spiritual and immortal soul he has no more moral dignity nor intrinsic worth than a horse, a cow or an elephant." [25] And the same writer then proceeds to add supernatural to natural dignity. There can be no objection to this adding of dignity to dignity. Man is in sore need of it. But these superadded dignities must not be allowed to obscure that dignity which is still man's whatever his relation to God or non-God, to a hereafter or a non-hereafter. There is a difference between Socrates, Marcus Aurelius, Jesus, Buddha, Confucius, St. Francis of Assisi, Thomas Aquinas, Shakespeare, Jefferson, or Lincoln and a horse, a cow, or an elephant which no conception of the universe, materialistic or spiritualistic, rational or supernatural, can make or unmake. Such men are to be accredited to the account of man in any appraisal of his worth. However superhuman, they are in any case human; their human qualities lend dignity to the race which may claim them as members. And lesser men derive dignity not only from kinship but from the sense of unworthiness. For perhaps man's greatest claim to dignity is his hesitation to claim it.

Natural dignity may even be enhanced by the absence of supernatural dignity, by men's capacity to bear themselves well merely as men. As André Gide has said:

> Men have gone to their death as martyrs although they had no dogmas to guide them and were supported only by their simple probity of spirit. It was a martyrdom without glory or hope of future recompense, and for that reason it was all the more admirable. Without following in their footsteps, let us say that human dignity, and the sort of moral carriage or *consistency* on which our hopes now depend, are capable of dispensing with the support and comfort of Faith.[26]

Religion adds faith to knowledge, hope to struggle, and love to reason. But the kingdom of man, even taken in its own terms apart from any kingdom of God, can add these virtues to the ancient virtues of courage, wisdom, temperance, and justice. The moral will is resolve, and not doubt or refusal—except refusal to abandon resolve or be stopped by doubt. It requires a faith in the future, even when supported by a knowledge of the past; it fills out the blank pages of ignorance with hope, lest they be written by despair; it raises the motive of human organization from necessity and convenience to love.

The new world order is to be an order of freedom, but there is a loneliness of freedom. The roof of one world, though it covers everybody, is a high roof, scarcely to be distinguished from the open sky. There are many who prefer the close embrace of tyranny. There is need of what a recent writer has called "escape from freedom." [27] The half-religion of human morality can mitigate this loneliness. Love does not consist merely, as Antoine de Saint-

Exupéry has said, "in gazing at each other but in looking outward together in the same direction. There is no comradeship except through union in the same high effort." [28]

The cause of a morally unified mankind on a physically unified earth is a "high effort." It seeks to achieve peace and fruitful co-operation not only among contemporary mankind, but between past, present, and future, the old and the new. It is as complex as it is wide and prolonged. It calls for the martial virtues, in combat against evil or against lesser good—against war, hate, prejudice, ignorance, and misery, against the complacency of partial success, and the disillusionment of partial failure.[29] It requires of mankind the sort of courage of which Churchill spoke when he said that "the true measure of nations is what they can do when they are tired." [30]

The ideal of a morally unified mankind has the attributes that an ideal should have in order to call human faculties into play at their maximum and best. It is not impossible, but attainable. It is not attainable soon, but in the long run, and meanwhile creates a sense of movement and direction. It is attainable, but not easily. It is attainable, but only by intelligence as well as by effort. It is not attainable by one man alone, but only by each man in association with his fellows—by divided labor and labor combined, to the end that all men may enjoy together what together they have had the joy of building

NOTES

FOOTNOTES TO CHAPTER ONE

1 Quoted by B. H. M. Vlekke, *Nusantara; A History of the East Indian Archipelago,* Harvard University Press, 1943, p. 117.

2 *Conqueror of the Seas: The Story of Magellan,* Viking Press, 1938, pp. 235, 294-95.

3 R. E. Harrison, *Saturday Review of Literature,* Vol. XXVII, No. 27 (1944), p. 6.

4 Cf. Julius Kaerst, *Die antike Idee der Oekumene in ihrer politischen und kulturellen Bedeutung,* Leipzig, 1903.

5 Quoted by Winthrop M. Daniels, *American Railroads,* Princeton University Press, 1932, pp. 10-11.

6 These statistics for railway mileage and ship tonnage are given in the *Encyclopaedia Britannica,* 14th ed.

7 Cf. Eugene Staley, *World Economy in Transition,* Royal Institute of International Affairs, London, 1939, p. 14. Most of the data on travel time have been borrowed from this book.

8 Clive Day, pp. 58-61.

9 *Ibid.,* pp. 270-71.

10 Staley, *op. cit.,* pp. 20-35.

FOOTNOTES TO CHAPTER TWO

1 Quoted by D. A. Maclean, *The Christian Basis for a New World Order,* reprinted from *American Journal of Economics and Sociology,* 1942, p. 419.

2 F. S. Churchill, *The Children of Germany and Permanent Peace,* reprinted from *Cape Cod Standard-Times,* May 28, 1943.

3 Reprinted from *American Journal of Public Health,* Vol. 34, No. 11, (November, 1944), p. 1138.

4 Pope Pius XII, *"Christmas Message,"* 1941, reprinted in Guido Gonella, *A World to Reconstruct, Pius XII on Peace and Reconstruction,* translated by T. L. Bouscaren, Bruce Publishing Company, 1944, p. 298.

5 *The Time for Decision,* Harper, 1944, p. 401.

6 Cf. John O'Grady, "Test of a Good Neighbor," *Commonweal,* Feb. 16, 1945, pp. 438-41.

7 Carl L. Becker, *The Heavenly City of the Eighteenth-Century Philosophers,* Yale University Press, 1932, pp. 39-40.

Notes

[8] The Abbé de Saint-Pierre, *L'État de guerre et le projet de paix per-pétuelle, par J. J. Rousseau,* ed. by S. G. Patterson, 1920, p. 23. (Translated by the Author.)

[9] Address to the House of Commons on Feb. 23, 1944, as reported in the *New York Times* of the same date.

[10] Shelley, *"Prometheus Unbound," Works,* Houghton Mifflin, 1901, p. 206 (Cambridge edition).

[11] Among recent books which recognize this many-sidedness of the present problem the following deserve special mention: George B. de Huszar, ed., *New Perspectives on Peace,* University of Chicago Press, 1944; Lyman Bryson, L. Finkelstein, and R. M. McIver, eds., *Approaches to World Peace,* Harper, 1944; John B. Whitton, ed., *The Second Chance,* Princeton University Press, 1944.

[12] For a disproof by an economist of the thesis that all wars are of economic origin, cf. Jacob Viner, "International Relations between State-controlled National Economies," *American Economic Review,* Vol. XXXIV (1944), Supplement, pp. 322-25.

[13] Arthur B. Hall, July 12, 1943.

[14] Cf. Margaret Mead, *And Keep Your Powder Dry,* Morrow, 1943, pp. 196-209.

FOOTNOTES TO CHAPTER THREE

[1] *Complete Works,* ed. by John A. Nicolay and John Hay, 2 vols., Century, 1902, Vol. II, p. 64.

[2] Immanuel Kant, "The Natural Principle of the Political Order. Considered in connection with the Idea of a Universal Cosmopolitical History," in *Eternal Peace and Other International Essays,* translated by W. Hastie, World Peace Foundation, 1914, pp. 14-15.

[3] *Ibid.,* pp. 1, 9, 11.

[4] Quincy Wright, *The Protection by International Action of the Freedom of the Individual within the State,* Universities Committee on Post-War International Problems, Problem X, p. 7. These freedoms are all taken from the Atlantic Charter or from President Roosevelt's Four Freedoms.

[5] A. Barr Comstock, *New York Times,* Feb. 11, 1945.

[6] J. B. S. Haldane, *Nation,* Oct. 3, 1942, p. 294.

[7] Nicholas Spykman, *America's Strategy in World Politics,* Harcourt, Brace, 1942, quoted in *Saturday Review of Literature,* Apr. 22, 1944, p. 31.

[8] George Catlin, "Britain and Europe," *Commonweal,* Vol. XXXIX (1944), p. 538.

[9] Walter Lippmann, *U. S. War Aims,* Little, Brown, 1944, p. 174.

[10] Cf. Charles G. Fenwick, *International Law,* Century, 1924, pp. 44-45.

[11] Quoted in the *New York Times,* Oct. 16, 1943. (Italics mine)

[12] Quoted in the *New York Times,* May 25, 1944.

[13] Cf. William T. R. Fox, *The Super-Powers,* Harcourt, Brace, 1944, pp. 95 ff.

Notes

FOOTNOTES TO CHAPTER FOUR

1 In this summary use has been made of Fenwick, *International Law.* Cf. also C. C. Hyde, *International Law, Chiefly as Interpreted and Applied by the United States,* Little, Brown, 1922.

2 *Eternal Peace and Other International Essays,* p. 83.

3 *New York Times,* Feb. 6, 1945.

4 *New Yorker,* Apr. 15, 1944, p. 46.

5 "The Principle of Progress," *op. cit.,* p. 65.

6 Cf. Manley Hudson, "The International Law of the Future," *International Conciliation,* Carnegie Endowment for International Peace, December 1944, p. 767.

7 *War and the Working Class,* as quoted in the *New York Times,* Jan. 7, 1945. Cf. also *Information Bulletin,* published by the Soviet Embassy in Washington, Dec. 5, 1944, pp. 1-2.

8 Printed and distributed by Americans United for World Organization, Inc., New York City.

9 Cf. Quincy Wright, *Human Rights and the World Order,* Commission to Study the Organization of Peace, 1942; and his *The Protection by International Action of the Freedom of the Individual within the State,* Universities Committee on Post-War International Problems.

10 Cf. John Westlake, *Chapters on the Principles of International Law,* Cambridge University Press, 1894, Chap. II.

11 Fenwick, *op. cit.,* pp. 83-84.

12 For an excellent discussion of this subject, cf. Westlake, *op. cit.,* Chap. VII.

13 Cf. Fenwick, *op. cit.,* pp. 22-23.

FOOTNOTES TO CHAPTER FIVE

1 From a resolution adopted at the convention of the N.A.M. as reported in the *New York Times,* Dec. 8, 1944.

2 From an address quoted in the *Boston Herald,* Apr. 28, 1943.

3 Cf. Staley, *World Economy in Transition,* Pts. I, II.

4 *Ibid.,* pp. 24-35.

5 Adolph M. Lowe, *The Study of World Affairs,* published for the Institute of World Affairs by the Oxford University Press, 1944.

6 Cf. Staley, *op. cit.,* pp. 30-35.

7 On the noneconomic causes of war, cf. Jacob Viner, "The Economic Problem," in Huszar, ed., *New Perspectives on Peace.*

8 Cf. Gabriel Javsicas, *Shortage of Victory,* Appleton-Century, 1943, pp. 4, 6, and ff.

9 Kirtley F. Mather, "Economic Cooperation," second broadcast on the Six Pillars of Peace, Massachusetts Council of Churches, June 4, 1944.

10 Cf. John F. Timmons, *Free World,* April 1945, pp. 77-80.

Notes

[11] Cf. the resolution adopted by the International Labor Conference in Philadelphia, May 12, 1944, *New York Times*, May 13.

[12] Mather, *op. cit.*, pp. 3-4.

[13] Quoted in the *New York Herald Tribune*, Apr. 6, 1943.

[14] Cf. G. P. Marsh, *Man and Nature*, Scribner, 1865, pp. 326-29.

[15] *Annual Message to Congress*, Jan. 6, 1941.

[16] *World Trade and Employment: Report from the Advisory Committee on Economics to the Committee on International Economic Policy*, New York City, 1944. Cf. other pamphlets in this series; and J. B. Condliffe, *Agenda for a Postwar World*, Norton, 1942.

[17] *British Moralists*, ed. by L. A. Selby-Bigge, 3 vols., Oxford University Press, 1897, Vol. I, pp. 309-10.

[18] Edward H. Carr, *Conditions of Peace*, Macmillan, 1942, pp. xviii-xix.

FOOTNOTES TO CHAPTER SIX

[1] Cf. C. Kluckhohn and W. H. Kelly, "The Concept of Culture," in Ralph Linton, ed., *The Science of Man in the World Crisis*, Columbia University Press, 1945, pp. 78-106.

[2] The fundamental document here is Josef Stalin, *Marxism and the National Question*, International Publishers, 1942. Cf. also Hans Kohn, *Nationalism in the Soviet Union*, translated by E. W. Dickes, Columbia University Press, 1933; and Erich Hula, "The Nationalities Policy of the Soviet Union," *Social Research*, May 1944.

[3] P. O. Lapie, *Foreign Affairs*, Vol. 23 (October 1944), pp. 107-09.

[4] *The World of Yesterday: An Autobiography*, Viking Press, 1943, p. 140.

[5] *New Republic*, Nov. 22, 1943, p. 724.

[6] Harper, 1943, pp. 307, 321.

[7] *The Republic*, translated by Benjamin Jowett, Oxford University Press, 1897, Bk. III, p. 399.

[8] B. Stallare, "The Revenge of Norway," *Free World*, March 1945, pp. 52-53.

[9] *Op. cit.*, p. 139.

[10] "*Demander la victoire et n'avoir pas envie de se battre, je trouve que c'est mal élevé,*" *Prose and Poetry*, translated by Ann and Julian Green, Pantheon Books, 1943, p. 165.

[11] W. H. Auden, "Henry James and the Dedicated," *New York Times*, Dec. 17, 1944, Book Review Section, p. 3.

[12] *Art*, Stokes, 1913, pp. 252, 274-75.

[13] G. P. Murdock, "The Common Denominator of Cultures," in Linton, *op. cit.*, pp. 124-25.

[14] Willard Price, *Japan's Islands of Mystery*, John Day, 1944, pp. 171-72.

[15] *Paideia*, Vol. I, pp. 310-11.

[16] *Diuturna*, Milano, 1924, pp. 374-77 ("*Relativismo e Fascismo*"); quoted by Franz Neumann, *Behemoth, The Structure and Practice of National Socialism*, Oxford University Press, 1942, pp. 462-63.

[17] *Paideia*, Vol. I, p. xxiv.

Notes

[18] Unpublished "Memorandum on the Activities and Future Plans of International Scientific Organizations," prepared for the Division of Foreign Relations of the National Research Council by W. B. Cannon and R. M. Field.

[19] Sacheverell Sitwell, *Valse des Fleurs,* Ryerson Press, 1941, pp. 58-59.

[20] Both quotations are borrowed from W. H. Chamberlin, *Collectivism,* Macmillan, 1937, p. 236.

[21] Cf. Arnold M. Walter, "Music a Means to Unify Mankind," in Bryson, Finkelstein, and McIver, eds., *Approaches to World Peace,* p. 521.

[22] Cf. W. G. Constable, "Can the Arts Help toward International Unity?" in *Ibid.,* pp. 494-95.

FOOTNOTES TO CHAPTER SEVEN

[1] Cf. *Education and World Peace, Problem Analysis Prepared for the Universities Committee on Post-War International Problems,* Boston, 1943; and the divers pamphlets and memoranda issued by the Committee on Education and Cultural Relations of the American Council on Education, by the Educational Policies Commission of the National Educational Association and the American Association of School Administrators, and by various other bodies.

[2] Charles W. Eliot, *The Cultivated Man,* Houghton Mifflin, 1909, p. 4.

[3] W. T. Van Stockum, *Commonweal,* Jan. 26, 1945, p. 372.

[4] *International Affairs,* January 1944, pp. 9-10.

[5] Joseph Glanvill, *The Vanity of Dogmatizing* (facsimile text), Columbia University Press, 1931, p. 183.

[6] Those who regard Nazism as a superficial and passing vagary would do well to read the studies of the German mind made during and after the First World War, and note the extent to which the symptoms, diagnosis, and prognosis of 1914–18 resemble those of 1945. Friedrich von Hügel's *The German Soul in Its Attitude towards Ethics and Christianity,* Dutton, 1916, is especially recommended. Cf. also the Author's *The Present Conflict of Ideals,* Longmans, Green, 1922, Chaps. XXVII, XXVIII.

[7] Cf., for example, Margaret Mead, *And Keep Your Powder Dry,* Chaps. XIII, XIV.

[8] Reported to me by the late Dr. C. Macfie Campbell.

[9] *Essays, First Series,* "History," 1884, pp. 10-11.

FOOTNOTES TO CHAPTER EIGHT

[1] Issued by the Commission to Study the Bases of a Just and Durable Peace, and adopted Dec. 11, 1942.

[2] Cf. Paul Hutchinson, *From Victory to Peace,* Willett, Clark, 1943, Appendix; Philip Hughes, ed., *The Popes' New Order . . . from Leo XIII to Pius XII,* Macmillan, 1944.

Notes

[3] From a *Bishops' Statement on International Order,* published in November 1944 by the National Catholic Welfare Conference.

[4] As reported in the *New York Times,* Nov. 14, 1943.

[5] Cf. *New Yorker,* Feb. 24, 1945, p. 20.

[6] Cf. Vlekke, *Nusantara,* pp. 72-73.

[7] J. J. Considine, *Catholic Action, Commonweal,* Nov. 3, 1944. When atonement and salvation are conceived as limited, their limitations do not coincide with differences of race, nation, or class.

[8] Hutchinson, *op. cit.,* p. 191. Cf. also the late Archbishop of Canterbury's (William Temple) remarkable and widely read *Christianity and the Social Order,* Penguin Books, 1942.

[9] Hutchinson, *op. cit.,* p. 194.

[10] *Ibid.,* p. 206.

[11] Gonella, *A World to Reconstruct;* Hughes, *op. cit.,* p. 298 and *passim.*

[12] An excellent summary of these changes is to be found in Charles S. Braden, *Modern Tendencies in World Religions,* Macmillan, 1933.

[13] *Ibid.,* p. 179.

[14] Cf. "Summary of Neo-Confucianism," in *Ibid.,* p. 118.

[15] Cf. G. I. Haight and C. H. Lorch, "Freedom of Religion," *Bill of Rights Review,* 1942, pp. 111-18.

[16] V. W. Rotnem and F. G. Folsom, Jr., "Recent Restrictions upon Religious Liberty," *American Political Science Review,* Vol. XXXVI (1942), p. 1054.

[17] Cf. Zechariah Chafee, *The Inquiring Mind,* Harcourt, Brace, 1928, p. 108 ff.

[18] For a summary of decisions and appraisal of tendencies, cf. A. W. Scott, *Harvard Law Review,* Vol. XXXI (1917–18), pp. 289-93.

[19] Haight and Lorch, *op. cit.,* p. 112.

[20] *Works,* 3 vols., London, 1851, Vol. I, p. 41.

[21] *Rights of Man and Natural Law,* translated by Doris C. Anson, Scribner, 1943, p. 21.

[22] J. C. Murray, *The Pattern for Peace and the Papal Peace Program,* Catholic Association for International Peace, 1944, pp. 7-8. For a fuller discussion of the present topic, cf. the Author's "Catholicism and Modern Liberalism," *Proceedings of the American Catholic Philosophical Association,* 1943.

[23] Cf. W. Parsons and J. C. Murray, *Intercredal Cooperation,* Catholic Association for International Peace, 1943, p. 26 and *passim.*

[24] Encyclical of Pius XII, Oct. 20, 1939. H. C. Koenig, *Papal Peace Mosaic,* Catholic Association for International Peace, 1944, p. 47.

[25] John A. Ryan, *New Republic,* Sept. 20, 1943, p. 396.

[26] *Imaginary Interviews,* Knopf, 1944, p. 107.

[27] Cf. Erich Fromm's book, which bears that title, already cited.

[28] *Wind, Sand and Stars,* Reynal and Hitchcock, 1939, p. 288.

[29] Cf. Harlow Shapley, "A Design for Fighting," *American Scholar,* 1944–45, pp. 19-32.

[30] Quoted by Carr, *Conditions of Peace,* p. xxiv.

INDEX

Index

Index